Creative Ideas for Pastoral Liturgy

BAPTISM, CONFIRMATION and LITURGIES FOR THE JOURNEY

Jan Brind is a wife, mother and pastoral musician. She is a member of the Diocesan Worship Committee in Guildford, and a pastoral assisant at St Andrew's Church, Cobham. She helps run workshops and facilitate music days which encourage parishes to use new songs and be creative with liturgy.

Tessa Wilkinson is a wife, mother, grandmother, artist and counsellor. She passionately believes that everyone can be, and should be, creative. Over the years she has lived and worked in many different parishes and enjoyed encouraging others to discover their creative gifts. She now lives in London.

Creative Ideas for Pastoral Liturgy

Baptism, Confirmation and Liturgies for the Journey

Jan Brind and Tessa Wilkinson

CANTERBURY PRESS
Norwich

© Jan Brind and Tessa Wilkinson 2010

First published in 2010 by the Canterbury Press Norwich
Editorial office
13–17 Long Lane,
London, EC1A 9PN, UK

Canterbury Press is an imprint of Hymns Ancient and Modern Ltd (a
registered charity)
St Mary's Works, St Mary's Plain,
Norwich, NR3 3BH, UK

www.scm-canterburypress.co.uk

British Library Cataloguing in Publication data

A catalogue record for this book is available
from the British Library

978-1-84825-004-8

Typeset by Regent Typesetting, London
Printed and bound in Great Britain by
CPI Antony Rowe, Chippenham, Wiltshire

This book is dedicated with love to
Ted, Erica, Pat, Mich, Sally and Simon
who have supported and encouraged us
and who continue to share our life's journey

CONTENTS

INTRODUCTION

This is the third in a set of three books giving creative ideas for pastoral liturgy. *Marriage Services, Wedding Blessings and Anniversary Thanksgivings* was published in early 2009, and *Funeral, Thanksgiving and Memorial Services* was published in 2008.

This third book is essentially a book about our Christian journey – about our belonging to and being members of God's family. It is about our active involvement in the life of that family in the context of the Church. It is about celebrating and affirming each other and rejoicing in the gifts which God our Father has graciously given to each one of us. God sent his Son Jesus to show us the way and to teach us how to live – so this book is also about being the body of Christ, and sharing his love with those around us.

Our Christian journey begins with holy baptism. The authorized baptism liturgy given in *Common Worship* is beautiful. We have 'walked' through the liturgy and suggested some ideas to add to it – altar frontals, a wrapping shawl, a children's puzzle sheet, a bag for life, anniversary cards and more. There are then some ideas to go alongside confirmation including banners, named candles, a tile cross and white stones, cards and certificates.

As we journey on in our faith, as our stories unfold, and as members of our local parish churches, we often become involved in all sorts of activities – things that make up the mission and meaning of our faith and cement our relationships with others. We might belong to a group that arranges flowers in the church, or we might sing in the choir, or be on the Parochial Church Council (PCC) helping to make decisions on behalf of the people of God in that place, or work with children and young people, or pour the coffee – or, indeed, be on the ministry team in an authorized role. We all have gifts to offer and a ministry to share with others. And these gifts and ministries need to be celebrated and affirmed – often! People do need to be thanked sometimes for the things they do for others. These are often things in the background, which people may not see or be aware of much of the time unless they stop to consider. It is quite an eye opener to make a list of all the people who are involved in the church's life in one way or another. Their lives and gifts, taken as a whole, intertwined and woven together, make up the living fabric of the church. We have given resources to celebrate and say thank you to many of the individuals and groups that are found in most churches.

Then there are the welcomes and farewells. People come and go in a church congregation. Members of our ministry teams change and we have to say good-bye sometimes to people we may have grown to love, in the broadest sense, and we welcome new ones to take their place. Others, as part of their training, spend a period of time with us. Our young people leave to go travelling or to continue education elsewhere for a while. Groups go on pilgrimage, and so on. These are all occasions that can be acknowledged – they are markers on our shared journey as Christians. It is good sometimes to think 'outside the box' and to do something different. We have given some ideas for saying hello and farewell.

There is a house blessing, and some resources for a service of thanksgiving and dedication for a new building or re-ordered church. Sometimes a church has to be closed, for various reasons, and we have thought about this and have come up with some suggestions for marking what is often a painful and difficult time of ending and new beginning.

As in all our books, we have given instructions for making, among other things, altar frontals, banners and stoles, for decorating candles and making bags for life. We have listed resource books that might be helpful, hymn books and song books, and a list of appropriate hymns and songs to accompany the journey. We again remind everyone that many of the songs we suggest are not necessarily cov-ered by a Christian Copyright Licence (www.ccli.co.uk) but may be covered by a Calamus Licence (www.decanimusic.co.uk). One of the things we hope we are always encouraging people to do is to discover some of the new songs that are being composed today by very gifted pastoral musicians.

A CD containing all the material in this book is included. This allows you to download and use any bits you may want. As always, please feel free to change the words and make them appropriate to your particular situation. We do ask, though, that you acknowledge our copyright on words and artwork that are ours.

And, finally, please enjoy this book! We have enjoyed writing it. We hope you will want to celebrate all the people around you and the gifts they offer. From baptism to confirmation, as adopted members of God's family, as we share the journey and walk together, there is much to do and much to be thankful for.

Jan Brind and
Tessa Wilkinson

HOLY BAPTISM

Baptism is a sacrament and, by water and the Spirit, marks the start of our Christian faith journey. At baptism we accept an invitation from God who loves us and calls us to 'die to sin and rise to new life in Christ' – our old life of darkness, without Christ, is over and we turn to a new life of light, *with* Christ. We make a decision to 'turn to Christ', are signed with the cross of Christ, are washed clean in water, sometimes 'clothed' in new white garments to literally 'put on Christ', anointed with oil as a symbol of the outpouring of God's Holy Spirit, and given a lighted candle as a symbol of the light that has come into our lives. At our baptism we are welcomed into the family of the Christian Church as its newest brother or sister, and we remain part of the family of the baptized people of God for the rest of our lives. We now belong to Christ – and '*Christ*ening' is a word often used by people who are really referring to 'baptism'.

At our baptism, if we are too young to make our own decision to accept God's invitation, others – our parents, godparents and sponsors – make a decision on our behalf. It is important that our parents, godparents and sponsors themselves understand that they, too, are on a continuing journey of faith and are able to demonstrate by example what it is to live as a Christian. As we are being welcomed into the family of the Church, it is important that other members of this family are present – baptism should take place during a service where the most people are gathered. The gathered people promise to support and pray for the new members of the family as they start their Christian journey. Later on, if we wish, at confirmation we confirm for ourselves the decision made on our behalf at our baptism.

Here, we are assuming that the candidate for baptism is a young child who is unable to answer for *him/herself* – though, with older children and adults coming to baptism in growing numbers, many of these creative ideas can be adapted appropriately.

CREATIVE IDEAS

The baptism liturgy is full of symbols and action. Make the most of these. Communicate power and meaning of symbols to everyone present – this is an opportunity for mission. We are more likely to learn from 'doing' than we are from 'watching'. We are all witness to, and part of, the beginning of the Christian journey for this newest member of the family of the Church.

Decorating the Church

Decorate the church for baptism. This is a 'birthday' in a very real sense and the church can do much to create a welcome and make the day even more special for the child being baptized. Make an altar frontal or banner with the words 'We welcome you' *(see design on page 23*. The child's name might be added *(see How to Make on pages 196–200)*. String a bunting banner across the church with words 'N, We Welcome You' *(see How to Make on pages 202–4)*.

Stole

Make a special stole for the minister to wear at baptisms *(see How to Make on page 211)*.

Service Sheet

If a service sheet is being used there might be a photograph on the front of the child being baptized. Alternatively, if the service is screen-based there might be a photograph on the screen. But do make sure that you have permission from the family to use a photograph in this way.

Guides for Children

It might be a good idea to invest in some baptism booklets for children so that children in the congregation can look at them with the help of adults, and visiting children can feel more informed about what is going on in the service. *My Baptism Book – A Child's Guide to Baptism* by Diana Murrie is one such booklet. Church House Publishing produce a children's Baptism Cube *(see Resource Books on pages 232–5)* A worksheet is a good idea too *(see design on page 14)*.

Movement and Light

The baptism liturgy is full of movement. The baptismal party are invited to the front of the church to be presented to the congregation then, as the liturgy unfolds, they move to the font, then back to the front, and finally they are sent out with a blessing. Make a trail of paper footprints *(see designs on pages 36–7)* around the church following the liturgy and leading the baptismal party on the journey of baptism. Ask a group of baptized children to help with the 'moving'. This will give a sense of pilgrimage – we are all on a journey with Jesus. A small group of children may each carry a lantern with candles lit from the Paschal Candle, the 'Light of Christ'. They can collect the child, the parents, godparents and sponsors, and lead them to the front of the church. They can then lead them to the font for the baptism and return to the front. During the 'Welcome' they can lead them around the church to meet the congregation. At the end of the service they can lead the procession out of the church, with the newly baptized child adding *his/her* newly lit candle to the light.

Presentation of the Candidates

The baptismal party – child, parents, godparents and sponsors – gathers at the front of the church with the minister. Ask any children in the congregation to join them so that they can see what is happening.

The minister addresses the congregation and asks them if they will welcome the child and *'uphold them in their new life in Christ'*. The congregation responds, *'With the help of God, we will.'* The minister addresses the parents and godparents of the child, asking for their commitment to pray for, and walk with, the child on *his/her* journey of faith, and they respond, *'With the help of God, we will.'*

The Decision

A large candle (the Paschal Candle) is now lit. *'In baptism, God calls us out of darkness into his marvellous light.'* The parents, godparents and sponsors now make, on behalf of the child, an important statement about their faith. There are three questions about turning *away* from sin and three questions about turning *towards* Christ.

Signing with the Cross

The sign of the cross is made by the minister on the forehead of the child. *'Christ claims you for his own. Receive the sign of his cross.'* Parents, godparents, sponsors and children may also make the sign of the cross on the child. The cross is an invisible mark to show that the person is a follower of Jesus and belongs to him, and will not be afraid to stand up for the Christian faith. (If the Oil of Baptism is used, it is pure olive oil that has been blessed by the bishop on Maundy Thursday. Alternatively, the sign of the cross is made with Oil of Chrism immediately after the baptism.)

Prayer over the Water

The baptismal party moves to the font, all the people turn to face the font, and the water of baptism is poured into the font from a jug. This is a good opportunity to enlist help from a child. Ask the child to lift the jug high to allow the water to splash down into the font in an exciting and dramatic way. (Make sure the water is not too cold.) The Prayer over the Water is said by the minister. Alternatively, the Prayer over the Water might be sung as a hymn, either as a whole or in parts *(see the metrical version on pages 20–1)*.

The prayer gives thanks to God for the water which *'sustains, refreshes and cleanses'* all life. It speaks of the Holy Spirit 'moving' over the water at the time of creation, of the parting of the water for the children of Israel as they journeyed from slavery to freedom in the Promised Land, of the baptism of Jesus by John with water in the River Jordan, and of the 'anointing' of Jesus by the Holy Spirit as Messiah. Water has the power to end life – and also the power to bring new life. So we are not only 'drowned' with Christ in the water of baptism but also reborn, resurrected, to new life with him.

Profession of Faith

Baptism

The child is held by the minister and gently dipped in the water, or water is carefully poured over the child's head, sometimes with a shell (a symbol of Christian baptism which pilgrims used to wear). Alternatively, water can be used dramatically and generously. The child might be 'whisked' through the water, becoming quite wet! The word 'baptism' comes from the Greek word *'bapto'* which can mean 'to dip' or 'to plunge' or 'to wash'. Whichever way, the action happens three times. *'I baptize you in the name of the Father, and of the Son, and of the Holy Spirit.'* The people respond with a loud *'Amen'*. If the child is very wet, it is a good idea to have a towel ready for drying. The minister can splash water over the people to remind us of our own baptism and reaffirm that we *are* 'the baptized people of God'. We are all part of the child's new story and companions on the way. If the people have moved to gather around the font, as they return to their seats they might pass by the font and make the sign of the cross on their foreheads to remind themselves of their own baptism.

Clothing

Now is the time for the christening robe to be placed on the child. His or her life has changed. In fact, most baptism candidates are already wearing their christening clothes, or 'robes'. This is a shame as it misses the symbolic action of 'clothing' (in orthodox tradition the child is baptized without any clothing on at all so the ritual of 'clothing' is much more dramatic). *'You have been clothed with Christ. As many as are baptized into Christ have put on Christ.'* One way around this is for the minister to wrap the child in a special baptism shawl. This can be a simple square of white cloth and might have a blessing printed around the edge. The child is literally 'wrapped' in blessings *(see How to Make on page 205)*. The church may like to keep a selection of christening robes to borrow in different sizes and designs. A new christening robe can be expensive, and the idea that the same 'church' robe might be worn and passed down from generation to generation speaks of the 'family' of the Church in a very special way.

Anointing

If the sign of the cross is made now instead of after the Decision, the minister signs the new member of the family with oil as a mark of new life given by the outpouring of the Holy Spirit. Instead of a cross the *chi-rho* (the first two letters of the Greek word for Christ) may be used. Christ means 'anointed one'. Anointing with oil recalls the time when Jesus was baptized by John. Jesus was anointed by God's Holy Spirit. 'This is my Son, the Beloved, with whom I am well pleased.' Olive oil mixed with fragrant spices is used – this is the Oil of Chrism. *'May God, who has received you by baptism into his Church, pour upon you the riches of his grace, that within the company of Christ's pilgrim people you may daily be renewed by his anointing Spirit, and come to the inheritance of the saints in glory.'*
    The baptismal party then returns to the front of the church.

Commission

The Commission is given. For a newly baptized child unable to answer for *him/ herself* the whole Christian community, congregation, parents and godparents, are asked to 'help and encourage' the child so that *'he/she may learn to know God in public worship and private prayer; follow Jesus Christ in the life of faith, serve their neighbour after the example of Christ, and in due course come to confirmation'*. The godparents are given special responsibility for guiding and helping the child in the early years with the 'help and grace of God'. This is reinforced by the certificates they will be given *(see designs on pages 25–7)*

The Welcome and Peace

The new member of the Church family is introduced to those present.

The minister says, *'There is one Lord, one faith, one baptism: N, by one Spirit we are all baptized into one body.'* The people respond, *'We welcome you into the fellowship of faith; we are children of the same heavenly Father; we welcome you.'* Or the minister might hold the child up for all to see and declare, 'This is the latest member of God's family!' Or the minister might walk around the church carrying the child and praying out loud for it and for the family, encouraging others to do so at the same time. This can be a prayerful and moving moment before the Peace is introduced and shared, and the baptismal family return to their seats.

Prayers of Intercession

These might be led by the family, godparents and sponsors, or by the children, or by one of the church families.

The Offertory

Ask the baptism family with the child being baptized to take up the Offertory.

The Lord's Prayer

The Blessing

Giving of a Lighted Candle

The family are invited to the front of the church again at the end of the service after the blessing, and a candle is lit from the large candle (the Paschal Candle) and presented to the newly baptized child to signify that light has come into the child's life. *'You have received the light of Christ; walk in this light all the days of your life.'* The people respond, *'Shine as a light in the world to the glory of God the Father.'* The candle is taken home and can be lit at each anniversary of the child's baptism and at birthdays. You might put the child's name on the candle *(see How to Make on pages 209–10).*

The Dismissal

The Certificates

The child is given a Certificate of Baptism *(see designs on pages 25–6).*
The godparents may each be given a certificate *(see design on page 27).*

Photo Card

If you have made an altar frontal with the child's name, take a photograph before-hand and make it into a card. Ask the children in the church family to sign the card to welcome the new member, and the card can be presented to the child with the candle at the end of the service.

Milk and Honey

A little-known but powerfully simple and meaningful practice was documented by Tertullian at the end of the second century. After the new believers emerged from the waters during the baptism service, they were given milk mixed with honey to drink, undoubtedly representing the sweetness of the promises of God (*A History of Christianity*, K. S. Latourette, HarperOne, 1975, page 194). Baptism was an entree into the faith community, and this practice was reminiscent of the Israelites crossing the River Jordan into the Promised Land of milk and honey.

Jhan Moskowitz, Milk and honey: forms that reflect our faith
Taken from the website <www.jewsforjesus.org>

The Bag for Life

Make a Bag for Life *(see How to Make on page 207)* and collect items for the newly baptized child's journey of faith. A label *(see design on page 28)* can be attached to the bag listing the items. The label needs to list the items and say why a certain thing is being given. The bag can be presented at the end of the service and each item can be brought up by a different member of the congregation. The person announces what it is – 'a bulb that you might live a life of expectation' and then places it in the bag.

Items might include:

- A card to welcome you *(see designs on pages 29–35)*.
- A book of prayers for quiet moments.
- A Bible to learn about the word of God.
- A candle to light your path (the candle given at the end of the service).
- A packet of seeds (or bulbs) to live a life of expectation.
- Milk and honey for the journey *(see above)*.
- A postcard giving information about church activities.

Baptism Party

There is usually a party after a baptism. If the church has a hall, it might be offered to the family for the celebration. If there are church caterers, they might be asked to help with refreshments *(see Graces to use at a Meal after Baptism on page 22)*.

Anniversary cards

Many churches send cards to mark the anniversaries of newly baptized children. *(see designs on pages 38–42)*.

The quotes in italic are taken from *Common Worship: Christian Initiation*.

At a Baptism

From *Words by the Way*

ANN LEWIN

Jesus said, 'I am the way, the truth and the life.'

Before the name 'Christian' was used, in the early years of the Church's life, followers of Jesus were known as people of The Way.

As you grow up, and begin to discover what it means to live the Jesus Way, you might like to ponder these truths, which we who were present at your Baptism pass on to you.

First, you are precious to God (Isaiah 43.4). Nothing you can do, no circumstances of your life can alter that. You may turn away from God, but God will never stop loving you, and will always welcome you back.

Then, you have a relationship with the created world. 'Consider the birds,' Jesus said (Matthew 6.26). Look at the flowers, marvel at the wonders of the created world, and the sustaining power of God which holds them in life. Let them remind you of your value. But being chosen and special does not mean being spoilt. We have a responsibility to the created world, and your relationship with God will challenge you to care for all that is around you, and use it with respect.

That leads to your relationships with people around you. They also are precious to God, and people who are on the Jesus Way are called to treat others as people who are loved, honoured and precious like us.

There will always be people around you on the Jesus Way to encourage you as you join in worship, read the Bible and learn to pray and reflect on your relationship with God and the world. But deeper than that is the love of God sustaining you, and the energy and life of God's Spirit filling you, and the friendship of Jesus as he walks with us all on the Way.

Have a good journey!

TEMPLATE FOR A BAPTISM LEAFLET

(Here, on pages 10–13, is a template of a Baptism leaflet which was produced by the Parish of St Peter, Wolvercote, in North Oxford. We are using it with permission. Delete these bracketed words, put your church's name on the first page, print the four pages of the template off and ask children in the Sunday school to decorate it with pictures . . . a family, the priest carrying the child, the sign of the cross, the font, a jug of water, a dove, a candle . . . then make A5 folded leaflets to give to baptism families and visitors to the church to take home.)

HOLY
BAPTISM

Welcome to this service of Baptism.
This leaflet aims to explain briefly what Baptism
means and symbolizes.

Baptism is about celebration, thanksgiving and welcome.

Baptism is

- a *celebration* of the child or adult being baptized;
- a *thanksgiving* for their life and for all that God gives them and us;
- a *welcome* into the family of the Church, both worldwide and locally.

Through baptism we join a vast family spanning time and space. We commit ourselves to follow Christ and worship God within that family.

Baptism is about promises.

God promises
- *to hold the child or adult being baptized in his love and care;*
- *to pour his love upon them constantly;*
- *to give them his forgiveness and healing when they seek it.*

We promise
- *to help the person being baptized to grow within the Christian faith;*
- *to pray for them and to walk beside them on their Christian journey.*

If they are old enough, the person being baptized promises
- *to try always to live their life in the light of Jesus' teaching and example;*
- *to worship and pray to God regularly;*
- *to allow God to develop their faith and their trust in him.*

Baptism is God's promise that no matter what happens to us in life, no matter what we do in life, he will love us with a love that will never let us go.

Baptism is about symbols.

*The **water of baptism** is*
- *a symbol of our new birth into life with Christ;*
- *a visible sign of God's love pouring down upon the person being baptized;*
- *a visible sign of God's forgiveness, renewing them and transforming the mistakes they have made (or will make) into something new and creative – like water gradually smoothing jagged stones.*

*The **sign of the cross** made with the oil of baptism is*
- *a symbol that the person being baptized belongs to God;*
- *a symbol that they live and grow as followers of Christ;*
- *a symbol of the Holy Spirit guiding and strengthening them day by day.*

*The **lighted candle** is*
- *a reminder that Jesus is the Light of the World who passed through the darkness of death to the light of resurrection;*
- *a reminder that God's light overcomes every darkness;*
- *a reminder that God's love and light shine out of the person being baptized among their families and friends, and into the world.*

Baptism is a milestone on an unfolding journey with God into a richer, deeper way of living.

Please take this leaflet home with you if you would like to.

BAPTISM WORKSHEET

SPOT THE DIFFERENCE
Eight things have been changed.
Can you find them?

Can you break the code and read the message?

....

....

How many things can you see in the church beginning with the letter 'c'?

....

....

....

CHILDREN'S BAPTISM WORD SEARCH
Try to find 17 words connected with baptism

B	A	P	T	I	S	M	J	H
E	D	R	O	B	E	A	E	O
G	N	O	I	L	C	B	S	L
F	A	M	I	L	Y	H	U	Y
O	M	I	T	C	R	O	S	S
N	E	S	G	O	D	S	Q	P
T	N	E	W	K	V	Y	Z	I
L	I	F	E	W	A	T	E	R
R	P	C	A	N	D	L	E	R
G	O	D	P	A	R	E	N	T

Baptism, Candle, Cross, Family, Font, God, Godparent, Holy Spirit,
Jesus, Name, New Life, Oil, Promise, Robe, Water

BAPTISM WORKSHEET ANSWERS

CHILDREN'S BAPTISM WORD SEARCH ANSWERS

G	N	O	I	L	C	B	S	L
F	A	M	I	L	Y	H	U	Y
O	M	I	T	C	R	O	S	S
N	E	S	G	O	D	S	Q	P
T	N	E	W	K	V	Y	Z	I
L	I	F	E	W	A	T	E	R
R	P	C	A	N	D	L	E	I
G	O	D	P	A	R	E	N	T

Baptism, Candle, Cross, Family, Font, God, Godparent, Holy Spirit, Jesus, Name, New Life, Oil, Promise, Robe, Water

SPOT THE DIFFERENCE ANSWERS

BAPTISM WORD SEARCH

Try to find 76 words connected with baptism. Some are in bold to help you get started!

F	O	R	G	I	V	E	N	E	S	S	A	B	G	N	I	M	A	N	C	T	A
A	G	E	L	L	E	H	S	F	T	R	U	T	H	O	I	L	D	Y	I	Y	N
M	E	S	I	M	O	R	P	R	A	Y	E	R	E	I	H	E	L	R	T	J	O
I	P	U	X	J	P	L	E	H	B	A	P	T	I	S	M	O	I	R	K	L	I
L	A	R	Y	S	T	N	E	R	A	P	D	O	G	I	H	P	A	Z	S	O	N
Y	R	R	P	O	O	L	F	A	T	H	E	R	D	C	S	P	G	B	A	R	T
C	E	E	K	A	C	B	C	A	R	D	F	R	W	E	L	C	O	M	E	D	I
K	N	C	A	L	L	I	N	G	I	J	I	H	Y	D	O	B	D	E	G	E	N
L	T	T	M	N	O	R	F	O	N	T	P	R	E	F	R	E	S	H	I	N	G
T	S	I	R	H	C	T	V	S	E	U	H	G	N	I	H	S	A	W	S	R	Q
W	R	O	B	E	X	H	B	L	E	S	S	I	N	G	U	Y	W	Z	U	A	C
I	H	N	G	F	N	E	W	L	I	F	E	J	X	S	B	W	A	Y	P	D	E
C	O	M	M	I	S	S	I	O	N	G	K	H	E	I	R	S	T	J	P	V	L
L	H	O	J	E	D	E	V	I	L	N	H	J	O	U	R	N	E	Y	O	P	M
E	P	I	N	O	C	Q	P	R	I	E	S	T	R	S	U	L	R	L	R	I	H
A	Z	I	L	A	Y	R	E	N	E	W	I	N	G	Y	A	H	W	S	T	L	E
N	H	E	R	D	B	E	L	P	I	C	S	I	D	E	C	L	I	V	E	G	A
S	I	G	N	I	N	G	D	E	K	R	A	D	S	R	D	G	C	A	R	R	L
I	G	A	H	L	K	I	N	G	D	O	M	N	U	S	A	I	N	T	S	I	I
N	O	M	Q	A	P	E	A	C	E	S	I	H	B	D	Q	F	K	L	I	M	N
G	N	I	H	T	O	L	C	X	O	S	C	H	R	I	S	T	E	N	I	N	G

Anointing, Baptism, Birth, Blessing, Body, Cake, Calling, Candle, Card, Child, Christ, Christening, Church, Cleansing, Clothing, Commission, Cross, Dark, Decision, Devil, Disciple, Evil, Faith, Family, Father, Font, Forgiveness, Gift, God, Godparents, Grace, Healing, Heirs, Help, Holy, Image, Jesus, John, Journey, Joy, Kingdom, Light, Lord, Love, Milk, Naming, New Life, Oil, Parents, Party, Peace, Pilgrim, Pool, Prayer, Priest, Promise, Refreshing, Renewing, Resurrection, Rite, Robe, Saints, Seal, Shell, Shine, Signing, Sins, Son, Spirit, Supporters, Truth, Washing, Water, Way, Welcome

BAPTISM WORD SEARCH ANSWERS

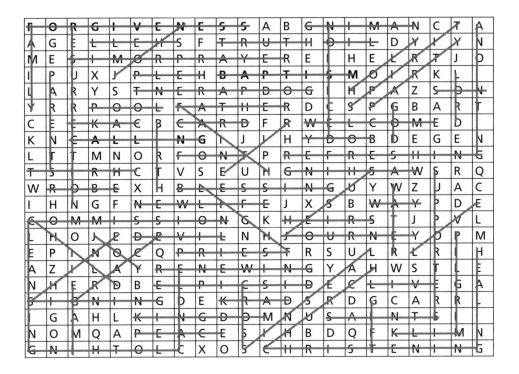

For the tasks which you are giving

Tune: East Acklam 84 84 88 84

1 For the tasks which you are giving,
Lord, count me in.
Christian love and Christian living,
Lord, count me in.
Take the fears that now impede us,
By your Spirit guide and lead us,
Help us know the way you need us,
Lord, count me in.

2 For the task of prayer and praising,
Lord, count me in.
Thankfulness for love amazing,
Lord, count me in.
As we take your Body broken,
As we hear your true word spoken,
May our wonder be awoken,
Lord, count me in.

3 For the task of love and caring,
Lord, count me in.
In this world your goodness sharing,
Lord, count me in.
In your life, and in your Passion
God most high, in human fashion
You have set us all the pattern,
Lord, count me in.

4 For your tasks our hands are lifted,
Lord, count me in.
Each of us uniquely gifted,
Lord, count me in.
Teach us, reach us, Lord inspire,
Spirit, set our hearts on fire,
May our song reach ever higher,
Lord, count me in.

Text © Andrew Body 1982

Gathered together to witness a birthing

Tune: Epiphany 11 10 11 10

1 Gathered together to witness a birthing,
   Water and Spirit to make all things new;
   Clothing, refreshing, reviving, anointing,
   Holy reminders of faith strong and true.

2 All who are lost in the shadows of darkness
   Now shall be bathed in your soft, shining light;
   God our Creator, you bring us to wholeness,
   Fit for your Church as the body of Christ.

3 Open our eyes so we see you more clearly,
   Sharpen our ears so your call may be heard;
   Widen our hearts so we love you more dearly,
   Make us a people who live by your word.

4 Jesus, our Lord, in his pain and his dying
   Carried our sin so that we may be freed;
   Rising again to give peace everlasting,
   Leaving the Spirit, as he had decreed.

5 Pilgrims rejoicing in Baptismal blessing,
   Formed by the Father, redeemed by the Son;
   Sent out to witness the Gospel unending,
   Led by the Spirit in whom we are one.

6 Given a new name, and strength for the journey,
   Claiming in Baptism promise foretold;
   This is our calling, and this is our story,
   God's living stones being Christ in the world.

Text © Jan Brind 2003

Prayer over the water

Tune: Finlandia 10 10 10 10 10 10

Here is a metrical version of the Prayer over the Water. It can be sung in different ways. The opening responses can be sung as below by president and choir. If the president is not a cantor, he or she can speak the president's lines while the Finlandia tune is gently played underneath, and the choir can sing their lines. This will give an introduction to what follows. The six line verses can be sung by all, or the choir can sing the first four lines of each verse and the congregation can sing the parts in bold.

The song might be sung in sections, the responses and first four verses as the baptismal party move towards and gather around the font, verses 5 and 6 at the font before the baptism, and the last verse walking back to the front of the church.

President	Praise God, who made the earth and all the heavens
Choir	**Who keeps his promise now and always will**
President	Let us give thanks to God our Lord Creator
Choir	**It's right to give him thanks and glorious praise**
President	All praise to God, whose promise is for ever
Choir	**All praise to God, we stand before you now**

1 Almighty God, we thank you for this water
   It gives us life, it cleanses and renews
   When you created earth and sea and heaven
   Upon the deep your Holy Spirit moved

   All praise to God, whose promise is for ever
   All praise to God, we stand before you now

2 When Israel's children journeyed out of Egypt
   And left their lives of slavery behind
   The waters parted leading them to safety
   And perfect freedom in the Promised Land

   All praise to God, whose promise is for ever
   All praise to God, we stand before you now

3 And in the waters of the River Jordan
   Our Saviour Jesus was baptized by John

The voice of God spoke through the Holy Spirit
Confirming Christ, his own beloved Son:

'This is my Son, the Chosen One, Beloved,
This is my Son, with whom I am well pleased'

4 As once again we follow where Christ leads us
From death of sin to risen life anew
We call to mind our faith and understanding
Declaring all that we believe is true

All praise to God, whose promise is for ever
All praise to God, we stand before you now

5 We thank you, Father, for this cleansing water
In it we die with Jesus in his death
By it we share in Jesus' resurrection
Through it the Holy Spirit gives us breath

And now in Jesus' name we sing a welcome
To those who come to be baptized in faith

6 Now sanctify this water by your Spirit
In it their sins shall all be washed away
And in new life, and bearing now your image,
The light of faith will always guide their way

All praise to God, whose promise is for ever
All praise to God, we stand before you now

7 May all your faithful people walk together
And share as one the risen life of Christ
And give to God, the Father, Son and Spirit,
All honour, glory, now and ever more

All praise to God, the Father, Son and Spirit
All praise to God, now and for ever more
Amen

Text of opening responses © Paul Jenkins 2008
Text of verses © Jan Brind 2008
(Based on the Prayer over the Water from *Common Worship: Christian Initiation*, Church House Publishing, 2006)

Graces to use at a Meal after Baptism

Praise God for *N*.
Praise God for welcome and celebration.
Praise God for bread broken and shared.
Praise God!
Amen

For oil to carry the sign of the cross,
For water poured to refresh and renew,
For candlelight to show the way,
For welcome into a new family,
For all these things we thank you, Lord!
And as we celebrate and break bread together,
may your love enfold us all.
Amen

Father, we are members together of your family,
And today we welcome *N* into our midst.
We rejoice and celebrate!
For this food and for all your blessings,
We give you thanks.
Amen

Heavenly Father,
We give you thanks for this food.
May we, who are blessed with such abundance,
Be mindful always of the needs of others
That our hearts and hands may reach out in love
To share equally that which you give to all people.
Amen

For today, for welcome and celebration
We give you thanks, Lord.
For this food, for laughter and togetherness
We give you thanks, Lord.
For tomorrow, for your love surrounding us
We give you thanks, Lord.
Amen and Amen

ALTAR FRONTAL OR BANNER

BAPTISM SERVICE COVER

THE BAPTISM OF

CHILD'S NAME HERE

DATE

NAME OF CHURCH

CERTIFICATE

CERTIFICATE OF BAPTISM

THIS CERTIFIES THAT

....

WAS

BAPTISED IN THE NAME OF THE FATHER & THE SON & THE HOLY SPIRIT

ON

....

AT

....

BY

....

CERTIFICATE

CERTIFICATE OF BAPTISM

THIS CERTIFIES THAT

....

WAS

BAPTISED IN THE NAME OF THE FATHER & THE SON & THE HOLY SPIRIT

ON

....

AT

....

BY

....

CERTIFICATE

COME HOLY SPIRIT

COME HOLY SPIRIT

I HAVE AGREED TO BE A GODPARENT TO

....

Baptised on..

at..

as a Godparent I have promised to:

Pray for them

Try to be an example to them

Walk with them in the way of Christ

Bring them to confirmation

FIGHT VALIANTLY AS A DISCIPLE OF CHRIST
AGAINST SIN, THE WORLD AND THE DEVIL
& REMAIN FAITHFUL TO CHRIST TO THE END OF YOUR LIFE

LABEL FOR A BAG OF LIFE

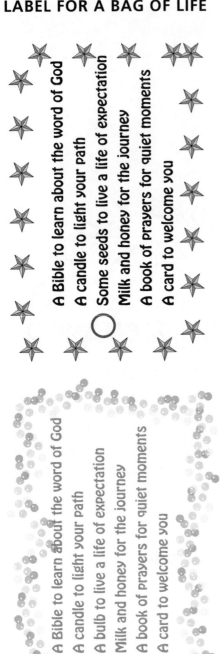
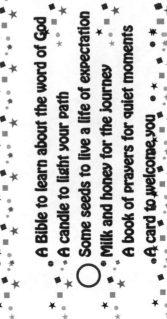

A Bible to learn about the word of God
A candle to light your path
Some seeds to live a life of expectation
Milk and honey for the journey
A book of prayers for quiet moments
A card to welcome you

A Bible to learn about the word of God
A candle to light your path
Some seeds to live a life of expectation
Milk and honey for the journey
A book of prayers for quiet moments
A card to welcome you

A Bible to learn about the word of God
A candle to light your path
A bulb to live a life of expectation
Milk and honey for the journey
A book of prayers for quiet moments
A card to welcome you

A Bible to learn about the word of God
A candle to light your path
A bulb to live a life of expectation
Milk and honey for the journey
A book of prayers for quiet moments
A card to welcome you

BAPTISM CARD

WE THANK YOU, ALMIGHTY GOD, FOR THE GIFT OF WATER TO SUSTAIN, REFRESH AND CLEANSE ALL LIFE

BAPTISM CARD

BAPTISM CARD

BAPTISM CARD

BY THE POWER OF THE HOLY SPIRIT BE CLEANSED & BORN AGAIN

BAPTISM CARD

BAPTISM CARD

BAPTISM CARD

FOOTPRINT TEMPLATE

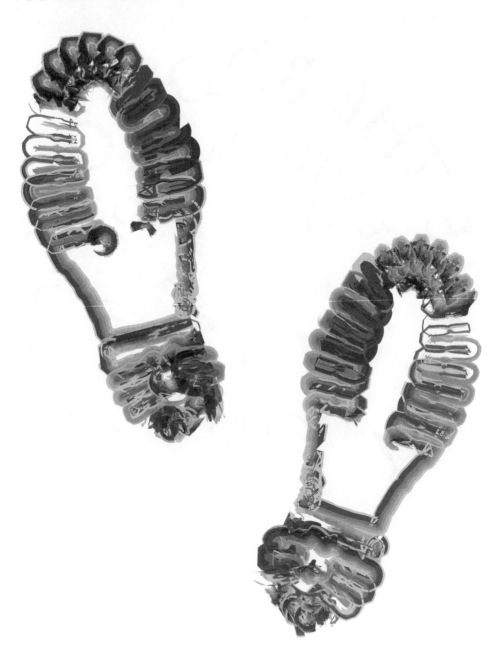

FOOTPRINT TEMPLATE

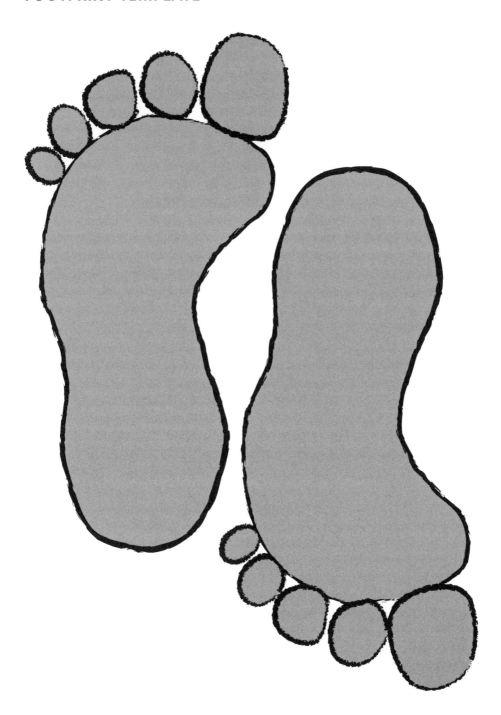

ANNIVERSARY CARDS

praise God for your
baptism
anniversary
1st

praise God for your
baptism
anniversary
2nd

ANNIVERSARY CARDS

ANNIVERSARY CARDS

praise God for your baptism anniversary

5th

PRAISE GOD FOR BAPTISM ANNIVERSARIES

ANNIVERSARY CARDS

PRAISE GOD FOR BAPTISM ANNIVERSARIES

PRAISE GOD FOR BAPTISM ANNIVERSARIES

ANNIVERSARY CARDS

PRAISE GOD FOR BAPTISM ANNIVERSARIES

PRAISE GOD FOR BAPTISM ANNIVERSARIES

RENEWAL OF BAPTISMAL VOWS

The renewing of baptismal vows outside a baptism or confirmation service should not happen more than once or twice a year at most. So it is worth making sure that when it does happen it should be something very special.

Once a year, hold a Baptism Sunday service and invite back to church everyone who has been baptized in the last 12 months. Suggest in the invitation *(see design on page 45)* that the family and godparents and sponsors might like to come back to the church to celebrate the baptism. Design a service around a baptism theme. Ask the adults/children coming to the service to bring their baptism candles with them. Everyone else attending the service can be given a small candle as they come into church.

CREATIVE IDEAS

Fill the font with water, if not already filled, and invite everyone to go to the font and make the sign of the cross on their forehead, or each other's forehead, as a reminder of their baptism.

After everyone has renewed their baptism vows, they can be given a card to take away to use in prayer and to act as a reminder of what they have said *(see designs on page 46)*.

At the end of the service, the light of Christ can be taken from the Paschal Candle and passed from candle to candle. Ask each person to use the wonderful words used in the Easter Vigil as they pass on the Christlight to each other, 'The Light of Christ', and the receiver of the light says, 'Thanks be to God'. Ask everyone to watch as the Christlight spreads through the church. At the Dismissal ask everyone to hold up their candles as the minister says:

May all of you continue to shine as a light
in God's wonderful, beautiful, mysterious world.
Go from here lit by Christ's light
Shine as a light in all you do, in all you say, in all you are.
Go! Shine!
Amen

Give a card with information about the church's children's work to everyone who comes with children. Give any visiting adults information about the groups the church runs and the times of the services.

After the service, serve refreshments. This might include a 'Christening Cake', or dove-shaped biscuits *(see recipe on page 47).*

Songs	**Father, we adore you (Fountain of life)** (*Songs of Fellowship*)
	Go peaceful, in gentleness (*Hymns Old and New: One Church, One Faith, One Lord*)
	Lord, I come to you (Power of your love) (*The Source 3*)
	This is the truth which we proclaim (*Sing Glory*)
	You have called us (*Share the Light*)
	You who dwell in the shelter of the Lord (On Eagle's Wings) (*Laudate*)

CELEBRATE BAPTISM INVITATION

YOU ARE INVITED TO

COME TO.......................... CHURCH

TO CELEBRATE BAPTISM SUNDAY

ON...

AT...

PLEASE BRING ALL THE FAMILY
PARENTS, GODPARENTS, GRANDPARENTS, BROTHERS & SISTERS

IF YOU STILL HAVE IT, PLEASE BRING YOUR BAPTISM CANDLE WITH YOU

ALL ARE WELCOME!

BAPTISM REMINDER CARD

WILL YOU CONTINUE IN THE APOSTLES' TEACHING & FELLOWSHIP IN BREAKING OF BREAD, & IN THE PRAYERS? WITH THE HELP OF GOD I WILL

WILL YOU ACKNOWLEDGE CHRIST'S AUTHORITY OVER HUMAN SOCIETY, BY PRAYER FOR THE WORLD & ITS LEADERS, BY DEFENDING THE WEAK, & BY SEEKING PEACE & JUSTICE?

WILL YOU PROCLAIM BY WORD & EXAMPLE THE GOOD NEWS OF GOD IN CHRIST?

WILL YOU PERSEVERE IN RESISTING EVIL & WHENEVER YOU FALL INTO SIN, REPENT & RETURN TO THE LORD?

WILL YOU SEEK & SERVE CHRIST IN ALL PEOPLE, LOVING YOUR NEIGHBOUR AS YOURSELF?

DOVE-SHAPED BISCUITS

Oven temperature 350°F (180°C) Gas Mark 4

Either use biscuit cutters or make dove templates to cut around for these biscuits.

Ingredients:

  100g (4oz) butter or margarine
  100g (4oz) caster sugar
  1 egg, beaten
  200g (8oz) flour

Method:

Grease two baking trays. Cream the butter and sugar until pale and fluffy. Add the egg a little at a time, beating after each addition. Stir in the flour and mix to a fairly firm dough. Knead lightly and roll out 0.5cm (¼ inch) thick on a floured board. Carefully place the templates on the dough and with a sharp knife cut around the shapes – or use dove-shaped cutters. Lift onto a greased tray and bake in the top of the oven for 15–20 minutes until firm and very lightly browned. Leave on the trays to cool for a few minutes before transferring to wire racks. The biscuits can be iced with glacé icing and sprinkles if you wish.
    This makes about 20 biscuits.

THANKSGIVING FOR THE GIFT OF A CHILD

When a child is born there is reason for much rejoicing and thanksgiving. Not very many years ago pregnancy and childbirth was an anxious time for a mother and child and, following a safe delivery, a mother would attend church where prayers would be said for her and thanks would be offered to God. There was also a belief that a mother was unclean until she had been 'churched' in this way.

Today, our thinking has moved on and the service of Thanksgiving for the Gift of a Child is just that. The service meets a pastoral need where baptism, for many reasons, is not the immediate choice of the parents, and it can take place in hospital immediately after the birth, at church, either as part of a main service, or in a small group, or at home. The same service can also be used for a newborn child as for an adopted child or a slightly older child. See the service of Thanksgiving for the Gift of a Child in the book *Christian Initiation* or *Pastoral Services*, part of the *Common Worship* liturgy for the Church of England, both published by Church House Publishing. It can also be seen on the *Common Worship* website. The service can be adapted to suit the particular pastoral need.

As part of the service, the child is welcomed with love, blessed and 'named', and friends or relatives are appointed as supporters for the child. This is not a baptism and these are not godparents, but they are concerned and trusted people who will be involved in the child's life, and may well become godparents if the child is later baptized. The child is given a copy of a Gospel, and a certificate to mark the occasion which must be kept safe.

Readings   At that time the disciples came to Jesus and asked, 'Who is the greatest in the kingdom of heaven?' He called a child, whom he put among them, and said, 'Truly I tell you, unless you change and become like children, you will never enter the kingdom of heaven. Whoever becomes humble like this child is the greatest in the kingdom of heaven. Whoever welcomes one such child in my name welcomes me.'

Matthew 18.1–5

People were bringing little children to him in order that he might touch them; and the disciples spoke sternly to them. But when Jesus saw this, he was indignant and said to them, 'Let the little children come to me; do not stop them; for it is to such as these that the kingdom of God belongs. Truly I tell you, whoever does not receive the kingdom of God as a little child will never enter it.' And he took them up in his arms, laid his hands on them, and blessed them.

Mark 10.13–16

CREATIVE IDEAS

The Giving of the Gospel

Use a bookplate to inscribe the Gospel with the child's name and the date of the Thanksgiving *(see designs on pages 52–3)*.

The Bag for Life

Print or sew the child's name on a cloth bag and fill it with special items to mark the Thanksgiving *(see How to Make on page 207)*. The bag can have a label listing the items. These might include:

- A book of Bible stories to teach you about God.
- A candle to light your path *(this might be named – see How to Decorate a Candle on page 209)*.
- A cloth to wrap you in blessings *(see How to Make on page 205)*.
- A CD of music to calm you.
- A card signed by your supporters.

The Child's Certificate

This might give the name of the child, the date and place of the Thanksgiving, the names of the parents and supporters, and the name of the minister who conducted the service. There might also be thanksgiving words *(see designs on pages 54–5)*.

A Supporter's Certificate

Give each supporter a certificate giving the child's name and the date and place of the Thanksgiving and the words, 'I receive *N* as a gift from God, and undertake to support and encourage *N* and *N's parents* with prayer and to surround them with love' *(see designs on pages 56–9)*.

THANKSGIVING BOOKPLATE

THIS BOOK WAS GIVEN TO

....

BY

....

AT A SERVICE OF
THANKSGIVING

ON

....

THANKSGIVING BOOKPLATE

THIS BOOK WAS GIVEN TO

....

BY

....

AT A SERVICE OF
THANKSGIVING

ON

....

CERTIFICATE OF THANKSGIVING

CERTIFICATE OF THANKSGIVING

THIS IS TO CERTIFY
THAT A SERVICE OF
THANKSGIVING WAS HELD ON

FOR

AT

PARENTS' NAMES

SUPPORTERS' NAMES

SERVICE TAKEN BY

CERTIFICATE OF THANKSGIVING

CERTIFICATE OF THANKSGIVING

THIS IS TO CERTIFY
THAT A SERVICE OF
THANKSGIVING WAS HELD ON

....

FOR

....

AT

....

PARENTS' NAMES

....

....

SUPPORTERS' NAMES

....

....

....

SERVICE TAKEN BY

....

SUPPORTER'S CERTIFICATE

SUPPORTER'S CERTIFICATE

I RECEIVE

_____

AS A GIFT FROM GOD.
I UNDERTAKE TO SUPPORT
& ENCOURAGE HER & HER
PARENTS WITH PRAYER
& SURROUND THEM WITH
LOVE

PLACE

_____

DATE

_____

SUPPORTER'S CERTIFICATE

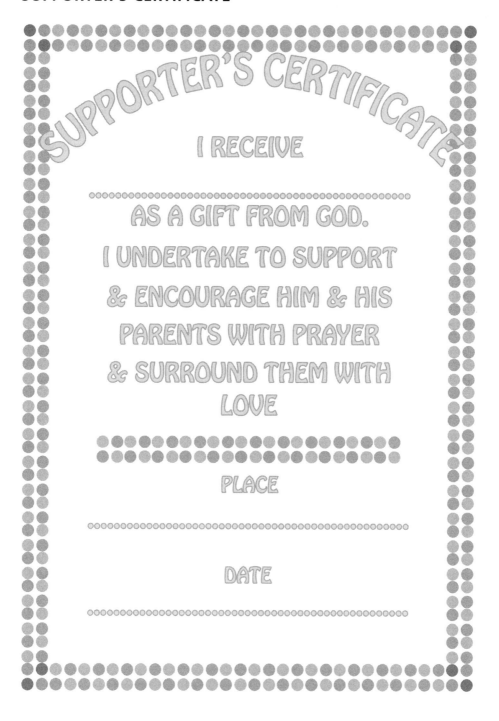

SUPPORTER'S CERTIFICATE

I RECEIVE

AS A GIFT FROM GOD.
I UNDERTAKE TO SUPPORT
& ENCOURAGE HIM & HIS
PARENTS WITH PRAYER
& SURROUND THEM WITH
LOVE

PLACE

DATE

SUPPORTER'S CERTIFICATE

SUPPORTER'S CERTIFICATE

I RECEIVE

AS A GIFT FROM GOD.
I UNDERTAKE TO SUPPORT
& ENCOURAGE HER & HER
PARENTS WITH PRAYER
& SURROUND THEM WITH
LOVE

PLACE

DATE

SUPPORTER'S CERTIFICATE

SUPPORTER'S CERTIFICATE

I RECEIVE

••

AS A GIFT FROM GOD.
I UNDERTAKE TO SUPPORT
& ENCOURAGE HIM & HIS
PARENTS WITH PRAYER
& SURROUND THEM WITH
LOVE

PLACE

DATE

CONFIRMATION

Being 'confirmed' in the Christian faith marks the time when a baptized Christian is ready to make his or her own decision to confirm their baptismal vows, which may have been made on their behalf when they were too young to speak for themselves, and to affirm their faith in Jesus Christ. Parents and godparents and sponsors who have walked the Christian road with them thus far will often be at the confirmation service to witness this transition. It is a special and joyful time.

A bishop will preside at a confirmation service and will ask God to 'confirm' the candidates by firstly invoking the Holy Spirit, '. . . *Let your Holy Spirit rest upon them: the Spirit of wisdom and understanding; the Spirit of counsel and inward strength; the Spirit of knowledge and true godliness. . .*', before naming each one, '*N, God has called you by name and made you his own*', and then laying hands on each head saying, '*Confirm, O Lord, your servant with your Holy Spirit.*'

The people are invited to pray for all the newly confirmed candidates saying, '*Defend, O Lord, these your servants with your heavenly grace, that they may continue yours for ever, and daily increase in your Holy Spirit more and more until they come to your everlasting kingdom.*' (All these words in italic are taken from *Common Worship: Christian Initiation*.)

Sometimes a candidate is baptized first and then confirmed, in the same service. At confirmation the candidate receives the bread and wine at the Eucharist, usually for the first time (although, increasingly, children are being admitted to Communion before confirmation following a time of preparation). During preparation for confirmation the person, often with others, will explore what it means to be admitted to full communion in the Church. There is obviously much to discuss here which is not in the remit for this book.

CREATIVE IDEAS

Photo Board

Display photos of the confirmation candidates on a board in the church so that the congregation know who they are and can support them and pray for them.

Altar Frontal

Design and make an altar frontal to use at the confirmation service *(see designs on pages 196 and 76)*.

Bunting Banners

Put the names of the people being confirmed onto bunting banners and string them up around the church *(see How to Make Bunting Banners on page 202)*.

Candles

Each confirmed candidate receives a lighted candle at the end of the service. The candles can each be named and be decorated with a dove *(see How to Decorate a Candle on pages 209–10)*.

A Tile Cross

Before the service, give each candidate a white wall tile. Ask them to write their name in the middle of it and to surround their name with the names of their parents and godparents. Permanent marker pens work well on ceramic tiles. When all the tiles are complete, and just before the service, lay them together on the floor in a prominent place in the church in the shape of a cross. After each candidate is confirmed by the bishop, they are given a lighted nightlight which they go and place on 'their' tile on the floor. By the end of the service there will be a wonderful lit cross on the floor, shining light on the names of all the people who have just been confirmed.

White Stones

'I will give some of the hidden manna. I will also give each of them a white stone on which is written a new name that no one knows except the one who receives it.'
Revelation 2.17 (from the Good News Bible)

After each candidate is confirmed they are given a plain white stone with nothing written on it. They have to decide what God would call them. They have declared publicly that they believe in Jesus as their Lord and Saviour. God has accepted them as a precious child, and wipes the slate clean to give them a new start, so in that new start they have a new name known only to them – a name very much says who we are, what is at the heart of our being. Their new name might be, for example, 'Child of God', 'Precious child', or 'Loved by God'. They can keep the stone as a reminder of their confirmation and the new start that it gives. The new manna might be understood to be the new nourishment they will be given when they receive the bread and wine at Communion. Each candidate can be given a card with the quote from Revelation on it *(see design on page 69)*. Their local community, members of the church family, or members of the youth club can sign the card with a message of blessing.

Footprints

Give each person a copy of the poem 'Footprints'.

Holding Cross

Give each candidate a holding cross. These crosses are shaped to fit comfortably in the hand and can often be bought from a Christian bookshop, either online or from the shop itself.

Prayer Cards and Bookmarks

This prayer is said in Morning Prayer from the days after Ascension Day until the Day of Pentecost (from *Common Worship*). It would make a wonderful prayer for those who have been confirmed. Make prayer cards to give to each candidate *(see design on pages 70–3)*.

> *As your Spirit moved over the face of the waters*
> *bringing light and life to your creation,*
> *pour out your Spirit on us today*
> *that we may walk as children of light*
> *and by your grace reveal your presence.*
> *Blessed be God, Father, Son and Holy Spirit*

You can also use words from the confirmation liturgy, or other appropriate words to make cards or bookmarks *(see designs on pages 70–5)*.

First Eucharist in the Parish Church

At a confirmation service the newly confirmed candidates are invited to receive Communion first. If they are confirmed in a church other than their own parish church, as is often the way if there is a deanery confirmation service, invite them to receive Communion first on the first Sunday that they attend their parish church.

Certificates

Present confirmation certificates to the newly confirmed people on the first occasion they receive Communion in their own parish church *(see designs on pages 66–8)*.

Parties

Arrange a party after the confirmation service – or after the first time the newly confirmed candidates receive Communion in their own parish church. A party can also be arranged to celebrate the first anniversary of the confirmation (*See Graces to use at a Meal after Confirmation on page 65*).

Testimonies

Ask the candidates to write a small piece about themselves to print in the parish magazine. This is a way to get to know a little better the newest confirmed members of the parish.

Responsibility in the Church

Invite those who have become full members of the Church through confirmation to help in the ministry of the church. There are all sorts of things that they might be involved in – for example, welcoming at the door, bringing up the Offertory, reading, leading intercessions, helping in the Sunday school or youth group, or cleaning the church, or being on the PCC! In this way they immediately become an active member of the body of Christ in their parish.

Journeying On Together

Invite the group who have been confirmed together to meet up regularly. They might take turns to host an evening at home. Or they might agree to do something fun once a month – have a meal out together, go to the cinema, go bowling, or the like.

Graces to use at a Meal after Confirmation

Praise God for food that nourishes!
Praise God for drink that refreshes!
Praise God for families gathered together!
Praise God for the blessings showered upon us this day!
Praise God!
Amen

As this cake is cut and shared,
so may our lives be overflowing with generosity and love.
Amen

As *N* starts this new journey today,
may *she/he* be nourished by food for the journey,
blessed by friends on the road,
and have an ever-present awareness of being loved by God.
Let us break bread together and celebrate!
Amen

As we have shared the broken bread
and drunk the wine in memory of our Lord,
so may we now eat and drink in celebration
of all that is to come.
Amen

For understanding and faith confirmed.
For bread broken and wine outpoured.
For a pilgrim people celebrating the journey.
For today and tomorrow and all that is to come.
We thank you, Lord, and praise you.
Amen

CONFIRMATION CERTIFICATE

CERTIFICATE

CONFIRMATION

THIS IS TO CERTIFY THAT

....

WAS CONFIRMED BY

....

ON

....

AT

....

PREPARED BY

....

DEFEND, O LORD, THIS YOUR SERVANT WITH YOUR HEAVENLY GRACE THAT SHE MAY CONTINUE YOURS FOR EVER.

CONFIRMATION CERTIFICATE

CONFIRMATION

CERTIFICATE

THIS IS TO CERTIFY THAT

. . . .

WAS CONFIRMED BY

. . . .

ON

. . . .

AT

. . . .

PREPARED BY

. . . .

DEFEND, O LORD, THIS YOUR SERVANT WITH YOUR HEAVENLY GRACE THAT HE MAY CONTINUE YOURS FOR EVER.

CONFIRMATION CERTIFICATE

CERTIFICATE

CONFIRMATION

THIS IS TO CERTIFY THAT

....

WAS CONFIRMED BY

....

ON

....

AT

....

PREPARED BY

....

GOD HAS CALLED YOU BY NAME

CONFIRMATION CARD

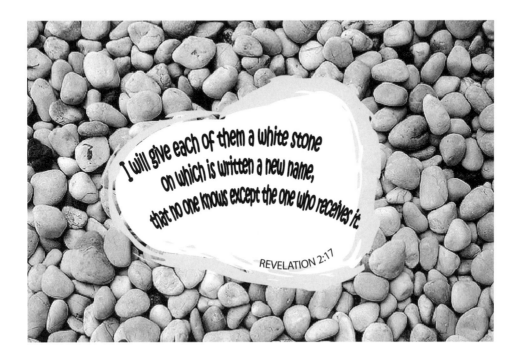

I will give each of them a white stone
on which is written a new name,
that no one knows except the one who receives it

REVELATION 2:17

CONFIRMATION PRAYER CARD

As your Spirit moved over the face of the waters
bringing light & life to your creation
pour out your Spirit on us today
that we may walk as children of light
and by your grace reveal your presence

CONFIRMATION PRAYER CARD

CONFIRMATION PRAYER CARD

Defend, O Lord, these your servants with your heavenly grace, that they may continue yours for ever, and daily increase in your Holy Spirit more & more until they come to your everlasting kingdom. Amen, Amen, Amen, Amen, Amen......

Defend, O Lord, these your servants with your heavenly grace, that they may continue yours for ever, and daily increase in your Holy Spirit more & more until they come to your everlasting kingdom. Amen, Amen, Amen, Amen, Amen......

Defend, O Lord, these your servants with your heavenly grace, that they may continue yours for ever, and daily increase in your Holy Spirit more & more until they come to your everlasting kingdom. Amen, Amen, Amen, Amen, Amen......

CONFIRMATION PRAYER CARD

LET YOUR HOLY SPIRIT REST UPON THEM:
THE SPIRIT OF WISDOM AND UNDERSTANDING
THE SPIRIT OF COUNSEL AND INWARD STRENGTH
THE SPIRIT OF KNOWLEDGE AND TRUE GODLINESS
AND LET THEIR DELIGHT BE IN THE FEAR OF THE LORD

CONFIRMATION BOOKMARKS

YOU HAVE BEEN
BLESSED AS
GOD'S
PRECIOUS
CHILD
now..............
GO AND SHINE
AS A LIGHT
IN GOD'S
BEAUTIFUL
FRAGILE
WORLD
and
MAY GOD'S
LOVE BE
BETWEEN YOU
and
EVERY PERSON
YOU MEET
TODAY
and
ALWAYS

YOU HAVE BEEN
BLESSED AS
GOD'S
PRECIOUS
CHILD
now..............
GO AND SHINE
AS A LIGHT
IN GOD'S
BEAUTIFUL
FRAGILE
WORLD
and
MAY GOD'S
LOVE BE
BETWEEN YOU
and
EVERY PERSON
YOU MEET
TODAY
and
ALWAYS

CONFIRMATION BOOKMARK

ALTAR FRONTAL FOR CONFIRMATION

Paint the background with sweeping colours.

Cut out the letters and stick on.

LITURGIES FOR THE JOURNEY

Celebrating the Bell Ringers

'Change' ringing began in the seventeenth century in church towers and has changed little since then. Bell ringers are a very interesting group of people! They come in all shapes and sizes, young and old, male and female, musical and non-musical, and are directed by a tower captain. They might be churchgoers or they might not. They might ring bells at several churches in one day, and they are often to be found at bell-ringers' gatherings far from home just for the joy of meeting other ringers and trying out other bells. Church bells are rung to call worshippers to church for a service. They are also rung joyfully after a wedding or tolled solemnly before a funeral. They are rung at the beginning of a new year and often, when the nation celebrates, bells can be heard ringing out the good news.

Thanksgiving   Lord, we celebrate and give thanks for bell ringers. By their dedication and skill the bells are brought alive to ring out their message. We give thanks for the bells that call us to worship week by week and mark the different stages of our journey. Their joyful ringing celebrates new life and marriage; their solemn tolling shares our sorrow in death. They ring in each New Year and proclaim good news when the nation has cause to rejoice. May the bell ringers continue to 'ring out the old and ring in the new' in the knowledge that they are much loved and valued members of our whole church family in this place.
Amen

Reading	Praise the Lord! Praise God in his sanctuary; praise him in his mighty firmament! Praise him for his mighty deeds; praise him according to his surpassing greatness!

Praise him with trumpet sound;
praise him with lute and harp!
Praise him with tambourine and dance;
praise him with strings and pipe!
Praise him with clanging cymbals;
praise him with loud clashing cymbals!
Let everything that breathes praise the LORD!
Praise the LORD!

Psalm 150

Dialogue

Two or three bell ringers might talk about how they came to ring bells and what it involves. Do they ring bells in other churches? Is it difficult? How do people learn to ring bells?

Blessing   Lord, send your blessing on these bell ringers.
May the ringing of bells continue to gather your people
in celebration and prayer.
Amen

Songs   **Come, now is the time to worship**
(*Sing Glory*)

May the peace of the Lord Christ go with you
(*Celtic Hymn Book*)

Over my head
(*Cantate*)

There's a spirit in the air
(*Common Praise*)

You shall go out with joy
(*Hymns Old and New: New Anglican Edition*)

The St Bees Bell Ringer's Hymn (1908)
(Canon H. D. Rawnsley
<www.stbees.org.uk/churches/priory/bells/pri_bel_ringerhymn. htm>)

Action

Encourage bell ringers to stay for the service (if they are not regular members of the congregation).

Take and frame a photo of the bell ringers and their tower captain to hang in the bell tower. This can be presented during the service.

In the weeks leading up to the service, ask children to cover bell-shaped 'medals' with foil. Thread ribbon through the medals and present them to each bell ringer during the service.

Share a cake and something fizzy after the service – decorate the cake with bells.

Ask the congregation to sign a card to present to the bell ringers at the service *(see design on page 80).*

CARD FOR BELL RINGERS

Celebrating the Bible Readers

Proclaiming the word of God is an important ministry in the life of the Church. From the Old Testament Bible texts we learn about God, God's law and the foundations of our faith, and in the New Testament we learn about the life of Jesus, what it means to follow him, and how to become a 'Christian'. So it follows that the word of God should be proclaimed clearly and truthfully by those trusted with this ministry. For those wishing to gain more insight there is a good handbook for readers Proclaiming God's Word *by Margaret Rizza published by Kevin Mayhew. At the end of the handbook is a useful guide to pronunciation of biblical names. Another book that Bible readers might also look out for is* Velvet Elvis *by Rob Bell published by Zondervan. This gives a wonderful fresh insight into how to read and discern the Bible for today.*

Thanksgiving   Lord, we celebrate and give thanks for our Bible readers. Through their ministry we hear the word of God proclaimed week by week. May the words that they speak bring salt and light to our hearts and minds, and may we so continue to learn and grow in spirit and in truth.
Amen

Readings   We who are strong ought to put up with the failings of the weak, and not to please ourselves. Each of us must please our neighbour for the good purpose of building up the neighbour. For Christ did not please himself; but, as it is written, 'The insults of those who insult you have fallen on me.' For whatever was written in former days was written for our instruction, so that by steadfastness and by the encouragement of the scriptures we might have hope. May the God of steadfastness and encouragement grant you to live in harmony with one another, in accordance with Christ Jesus, so that together you may with one voice glorify the God and Father of our Lord Jesus Christ.

Romans 15.1–6

I hope to come to you soon, but I am writing these instructions to you so that, if I am delayed, you may know how one ought to behave in the household of God, which is the church of the living God, the pillar and bulwark of the truth. Without any doubt, the mystery of our religion is great:

He was revealed in flesh,
vindicated in spirit,
seen by angels,
proclaimed among Gentiles,
believed in throughout the world,
taken up in glory.

Now the Spirit expressly says that in later times some will renounce the faith by paying attention to deceitful spirits and teachings of demons, through the hypocrisy of liars whose consciences are seared with a hot iron. They forbid marriage and demand abstinence from foods, which God created to be received with thanksgiving by those who believe and know the truth. For everything created by God is good, and nothing is to be rejected, provided it is received with thanksgiving; for it is sanctified by God's word and by prayer.

If you put these instructions before the brothers and sisters, you will be a good servant of Christ Jesus, nourished on the words of the faith and of the sound teaching that you have followed. Have nothing to do with profane myths and old wives' tales. Train yourself in godliness, for, while physical training is of some value, godliness is valuable in every way, holding promise for both the present life and the life to come. The saying is sure and worthy of full acceptance. For to this end we toil and struggle, because we have our hope set on the living God, who is the Saviour of all people, especially of those who believe.

These are the things you must insist on and teach. Let no one despise your youth, but set the believers an example in speech and conduct, in love, in faith, in purity. Until I arrive, give attention to the public reading of scripture, to exhorting, to teaching. Do not neglect the gift that is in you, which was given to you through prophecy with the laying on of hands by the council of elders. Put these things into practice, devote yourself to them, so that all may see your progress. Pay close attention to yourself and to your teaching; continue in these things, for in doing this you will save both yourself and your hearers.

1 Timothy 3.14—4.16

I warn everyone who hears the words of the prophecy of this book: if anyone adds to them, God will add to that person the plagues described in this book; if anyone takes away from the words of the book of this prophecy, God will take away that person's share in the tree of life and in the holy city, which are described in this book.

The one who testifies to these things says, 'Surely I am coming soon.'

Amen. Come, Lord Jesus!

The grace of the Lord Jesus be with all the saints. Amen.

Revelation 22.18–21

Invite all Bible readers present to come to the front of the church for a blessing and present each one with a copy of The 100-Minute Bible *and a bookmark.*

Blessing

May the Truth of God be in your speaking.
The Truth of God is our desire.

May the Wisdom of God be in your listening.
The Wisdom of God is our desire.

May the Holy Spirit of God be in your living.
The Holy Spirit of God is our desire.

May the Truth, the Wisdom and the Holy Spirit of God bless you as you continue to proclaim God's word in this place.
Amen

Songs

A lamp for my feet (Psalm 119)
(*Cantate*)

Alleluia! Raise the Gospel (alternative text)
(*Go Before Us*)

God's Spirit is in my heart
(*Hymns Old and New: New Anglican Edition*)

Listen now for the Gospel
(*One Is the Body*)

O Word of God
(*Cantate*)

Word of God
(*Cantate*)

Action   Give a bookmark to each Bible reader *(see design on page 85)*

Give a copy of *The 100-Minute Bible* to each Bible reader. This
was published in 2005 by The 100-Minute Press, Canterbury.

BIBLE READERS' BOOKMARK

Celebrating the Chalice Assistants

It is a great privilege to be asked to be a chalice assistant. Taking the consecrated wine and offering it to the congregation is a great honour. The following thanksgiving or celebration might be used when a new chalice assistant begins his or her ministry, or it might be used as a way of saying 'Thank you' to those who carry out this role in the church Sunday by Sunday.

Thanksgiving   Father, we give thanks for those in the congregation who have been selected and chosen to serve as chalice assistants in your church. As they carry this most precious gift of wine, consecrated and blessed, and given by you to all who will take it, we ask you to bless them and bring them great joy.
Amen

Reading   While they were eating, Jesus took a loaf of bread, and after blessing it he broke it, gave it to the disciples, and said, 'Take, eat; this is my body.' Then he took a cup, and after giving thanks he gave it to them, saying, 'Drink from it, all of you; for this is my blood of the covenant, which is poured out for many for the forgiveness of sins.'

Matthew 26.26–28

Dialogue

The chalice assistants might like to take a moment to tell the congregation what being a chalice assistant involves and what training they have had to do. At the end the parish priest might give them each a card expressing his/her thanks and the thanks of the congregation.

Blessing	'Jesus took the cup.' May God bless you as you lift up the chalice filled with consecrated wine. 'Jesus gave thanks.' May Jesus bless you as we give thanks for this most precious gift, offered to all. 'Jesus gave it to them.' May the Holy Spirit bless you and all those to whom you offer the chalice. And may the blessing of God, Father, Son and Holy Spirit, be upon you and all who receive the chalice from you today and always.
Songs	**Bread of life from heaven** (*Cantate*) **Broken for me, broken for you** (*Hymns Old and New: New Anglican Edition*) **Eat this bread** (*Laudate*) **Gifts of bread and wine** (*Complete Anglican Hymns Old and New*) **Here is bread** (*The Source 3*) **This is the body of Christ** (*Hymns of Glory, Songs of Praise*)
Action	Ask the congregation to sign a card for each chalice assistant *(see design on page 88)*.

CARD FOR CHALICE ASSISTANTS

Celebrating the Children's Workers and Youth Workers

Work with children and young people is one of the most important ministries in our churches. We constantly use the phrase 'Children are the future of the church' but sometimes we fail to grasp the fact that we need to make them feel welcome and wanted. So often we expect children and young people to 'fit in' with our comfortable and established ways of doing things – and then we wonder why they are reluctant to join us. On occasions when young people are fully involved in the worship, the whole dynamic of a church service changes – something happens and the worship comes alive. Young people today lead very visual and fast-moving lives – we have to listen to them and their needs and, most importantly, learn from them. Our children's and youth workers are introducing Christianity and 'Church' to young people in many different and innovative ways – and very often the 'future' of the Church is in their hands.

Thanksgiving Heavenly Father, we give you thanks and praise that you have called these children's and youth workers to bring the message of Jesus Christ to our young people. May they continue to nurture and teach our children by their example of forgiveness and love. We pray for each one of them as they do this important work as part of the body of Christ in this place.
Amen

Readings Then little children were being brought to him in order that he might lay his hands on them and pray. The disciples spoke sternly to those who brought them; but Jesus said, 'Let the little children come to me, and do not stop them; for it is to such as these that the kingdom of heaven belongs.' And he laid his hands on them and went on his way.

Matthew 19.13–15

Then he took a little child and put it among them; and taking it in his arms, he said to them, 'Whoever welcomes one such child in my name welcomes me, and whoever welcomes me welcomes not me but the one who sent me.'

Mark 9.36–37

I therefore, the prisoner in the Lord, beg you to lead a life worthy of the calling to which you have been called, with all humility and gentleness, with patience, bearing with one another in love, making every effort to maintain the unity of the Spirit in the bond of peace. There is one body and one Spirit, just as you were called to the one hope of your calling, one Lord, one faith, one baptism, one God and Father of all, who is above all and through all and in all.

But each of us was given grace according to the measure of Christ's gift.

The gifts he gave were that some would be apostles, some prophets, some evangelists, some pastors and teachers, to equip the saints for the work of ministry, for building up the body of Christ, until all of us come to the unity of the faith and of the knowledge of the Son of God, to maturity, to the measure of the full stature of Christ.

Ephesians 4.1–7, 11–13

Dialogue

Invite all the children's and youth workers to the front. Include all those who help with the teaching of children on Sundays and in youth clubs. Talk about the different groups, who they are for, when they meet and their activities. The following prayer might be said before they return to their seats

Prayer   For our children's and youth workers.
We praise you, O God.

For your message of forgiveness and love.
We thank you, O God.

For our children and young people.
We pray to you, O God.

For their energy and enthusiasm.
We praise you, O God.

For all that they teach us.
We thank you, O God.

For all that will be, today and tomorrow.
We pray to you, O God.

Blessing   May God, who calls each one of us to do his work,
bless us.
May Jesus, who calls the little children to his side,
bless us.
And may the Holy Spirit, who fills us with light and joy,
bless us and keep us, now and always.
Amen

Songs   Ask the young people to choose the songs for the service.

Action   Invite the different leaders to take an active part in leading the
service. They might be responsible for planning, welcoming,
reading, leading prayers, or even giving a talk or presentation
about something the young people are involved with.

If there is a young people's music group, invite them to play at
the service.

Invite all the young people's groups to decorate the church with
banners, bunting and ribbons *(see How to Make Bunting Banners on pages 202–4).*

Find out in advance something that the young people need, and
present this as a gift after the Dialogue.

Ask the children in advance to make and sign a 'Thank you'
card for the leaders – this might be presented by a child after
the Dialogue.

Celebrate at coffee time with a cake and fizzy drinks.

Have a display board with photos of people and events – this
might remain in a prominent place, being constantly updated,
so that everyone can feel involved in this part of the church's
life. Be careful to check that the families are happy for their
children's photos to be displayed.

Celebrating the Choir and Music Group

The choir and music group in a church are an ever-present and important part of a church service. Members are often committed to meeting for practice during each week so that in leading the congregation on the following Sunday the music is offered to the glory of God. The song or hymn words that we sing in church, and the music that accompanies them, have the power not only to teach us but also to lead and move us through the different elements of the liturgy. In particular, the words we sing become who we are, in that they inform our thinking and therefore the way we might choose to act. The director of music, or pastoral musician, in a church has huge responsibility to choose songs or hymns with words that are authentic and which tell the good news in ways that inspire and are remembered, and which send us out affirmed in a desire to live and work to God's praise and glory.

Thanksgiving   Lord, we celebrate and give thanks for the music in this place. We pray for the members of the choir and music group under the direction of N. We are mindful of their commitment to meet and practise each week so that they may support our singing, and so that the anthems, hymns and songs offered during our worship may be to the glory of God.
Amen

Readings   O give thanks to the LORD, call on his name,
make known his deeds among the peoples.
Sing to him, sing praises to him,
tell of all his wonderful works.
Glory in his holy name;
let the hearts of those who seek the LORD rejoice.

1 Chronicles 16.8–10

Be filled with the Spirit, as you sing psalms and hymns and spiritual songs among yourselves, singing and making melody to the Lord in your hearts.

Ephesians 5.18–19

Dialogue

Two or three members of the choir or music group might talk about how long they have been involved with the music in the church and what it means to them.

Prayer

We pray for your people, gathered in worship,
for word and for symbol, for sign and for space,
for voices raised in praise.
Lord, in our singing, may your story be told.

We pray for your church, both here and abroad,
for the good news of Jesus, and the life he proclaims,
for voices raised in peace.
Lord, in our singing, may your story be told.

We pray for your world, fragile and precious,
for green hills and oceans, for creatures and plants,
for voices raised in wonder.
Lord, in our singing, may your story be told.

We pray for your children, hurting or frightened,
scarred by injustice, or far from your light,
for voices raised in outrage.
Lord, in our singing, may your story be told.

We pray for your sick ones, waiting and hoping,
for patience and healing in times of despair,
for voices raised in intercession.
Lord, in our singing, may your story be told.

We pray for your saints, whose light goes before us,
for those nearing death, and the people who care,
for voices raised in hope of new life.
Lord, in our singing, may your story be told.

We pray for this day, and all our tomorrows,
for families and friends, for those we will meet,

for voices raised in love.
Lord, in our singing, may your story be told.

Anthem   *The choir may sing an anthem.*

Songs   Favourite or meaningful songs or hymns for the service might be chosen by members of the choir or music group.

Action   Take and frame a photo of current choir and music group members to hang in the choir vestry or in the church hall.

Share a cake after the service – it might be decorated with music notes and the words 'Celebrating Music'.

Organize a special 'Songs of Praise' evening.

Celebrating the Church Cleaners

There is one group of people who week by week do a job in the church that is often unseen and seldom given thanks for – the cleaners. Every building has to be maintained and cared for, and part of that maintenance is cleaning; dust, dirt and cobwebs collect in corners, under pews and chairs, on carpets and tiled floors. Carpets need vacuuming and floors need washing. Brass and silverware needs to be polished. Those who give up their time to make the house of God look at its best need to be thanked.

Thanksgiving   Lord, we thank you for this building that gives us shelter while we worship you.
Lord, we thank you for the people who have cleaned this church over many years.
Lord, we pray that as the care of this building is passed on from generation to generation, it may be a place of welcome and beauty, used to your glory.
Amen

Reading   They presented themselves and their brothers, consecrated themselves, and set to work cleaning up The Temple of God as the king had directed—as God directed! The priests started from the inside and worked out; they emptied the place of the accumulation of defiling junk—pagan rubbish that had no business in that holy place—and the Levites hauled it off to the Kidron Valley. They began the Temple cleaning on the first day of the first month and by the eighth day they had worked their way out to the porch—eight days it took them to clean and consecrate The Temple itself, and in eight more days they had finished with the entire Temple complex.

2 Chronicles 29.15–17 (from *The Message*)

Dialogue

Invite everyone who is involved in the cleaning of the church to come to the front. The person who runs the cleaning rota might speak about how the rota works and might take this opportunity to ask for more helpers if they are needed. Each person could then say their name and what they do. A card might be presented to the cleaning team and a small gift given to each person to thank them for all they do to keep the church clean.

Prayer   Praise God for all those who use dustpans and brushes.
We come with gifts both great and small.
We all make up the body of Christ.

Praise God for all those who clean windows and remove cobwebs.
We come with gifts both great and small.
We all make up the body of Christ.

Praise God for all those who vacuum and clean floors.
We come with gifts both great and small.
We all make up the body of Christ.

Praise God for all who dust and polish.
We come with gifts both great and small.
We all make up the body of Christ.

Those who clean windows and those who polish the brass and silver, those who dust and sweep and those who vacuum – each has a unique contribution to make towards the glorious multi-layered harmony of praising God through using their gifts, by keeping this building as a place of worship to the glory of God.
We thank you!
And we praise God!
Amen

The following prayers are written using some of the claims made on cleaning product bottles. They also fit very well with the claims we can make about God's forgiveness and the chance we are offered of a new beginning

A Flash™ prayer

Easy cleaning

Father God, we get it so wrong so often. In Psalm 51 it says, 'Purge me with hyssop, and I shall be clean; wash me, and I shall be whiter than snow.' Help us all to seek your forgiveness so we might be cleansed of all our sins. Your offer of easy cleaning is there for all to take.

All rooms

Father God, we pray that when we seek forgiveness for all the wrongs we have done we will explore all parts of our lives so that all the rooms within us will be cleansed.

Brilliant results

We know, Lord, that with your forgiveness we will get brilliant results and our lives can start anew, full of hope and joy.

Great fresh fragrance

As we go from here refreshed and cleansed, we pray we will be bearers of the fragrance that comes from knowing the forgiveness offered by our Lord and King.

A Cif™ prayer

Tackles the toughest cleaning jobs

We praise God that he forgives sinners again and again and that he will help us to tackle the toughest jobs of cleansing ourselves and starting anew.

It is powerful

Our God is all powerful and, with God at our side, there is nothing we cannot do.

It is versatile

Father God, we ask for help to be versatile and always open to your new ways and nudging. May we always be open to your Holy Spirit.

Leaves a brilliant shine

We pray that we will go out from here full of God's light, shining as lights in God's wonderful world.

A blessing   May the God of forgiveness and new beginnings, who sweeps us clean and allows us to start again refreshed and renewed, bless us.

May Jesus, our shining example, our guide and friend, bless us.

May the Holy Spirit who stirs us up, whirls us around and brings us back to somewhere new, bless us.

And may the blessing of God almighty, Father, Son and Holy Spirit, be upon us and all who take time to clean this church, today and always.

Amen

Songs   **I come with joy**
(*Hymns Old and New: New Anglican Edition*)

Take my hands
(*Be Still and Know*)

Take my life, Lord, let it be
(*Hymns of Glory, Songs of Praise*)

Take this moment
(*Iona Abbey Music Book*)

We are many parts
(*Laudate*)

You are the peace of all things calm
(*Celtic Hymn Book*)

Action   Give each cleaner a card with a personal message of thanks *(see design on page 99)*.

Provide a small gift for each member of the team.

A cake could be served with coffee after the service.

After the service, the cleaners might all go to the local pub and share a meal together.

CARD FOR THE CHURCH CLEANERS

PRAISE GOD FOR CHURCH CLEANERS

Celebrating the Churchwardens

To take on the role of churchwarden is a major commitment and therefore one that should be celebrated and given thanks for. Churchwardens are responsible for the 3 Ms (management, maintenance and ministry) in the church where they serve. It is a very important official position with their rights and responsibilities laid down in Church law. Every Anglican church will have wardens; they are the leading members of the lay church community. Sometimes it may feel a burdensome and time-consuming job needing a great deal of commitment and dedication but, if done well, it should be both interesting and rewarding. In an interregnum the role of the churchwarden takes on an even bigger significance and certainly when a new parish priest is appointed the churchwardens should be thanked for all they have done.

Thanksgiving Father, we give thanks and praise for our churchwardens. We pray that, as they work to further your good news here in this place, they will carry their responsibilities as parish officers and guardians of the parish church and its property with dignity and joy. We pray that the congregation will support them and help them in all they do, so the glory of God will shine out into the parish and beyond. We ask this in Jesus' name.
Amen

Thanksgiving after an Interregnum Before we look forward to our parish priest starting *his/her* new role here at St N's, let us pause and give thanks to God for the work done by the churchwardens during the interregnum.

For their time and dedication,
We thank you, Lord.
For their wisdom and discernment,
We thank you, Lord.
For their care of the church building and the fabric,
We thank you, Lord.

We ask God's blessing on the new journey ahead, that the team of churchwardens and the *vicar/priest/minister* and others who serve in this church will together find great joy and many blessings as they do God's work here in this place.
Amen

Readings

After they had proclaimed the good news to that city and had made many disciples, they returned to Lystra, then on to Iconium and Antioch. There they strengthened the souls of the disciples and encouraged them to continue in the faith, saying, 'It is through many persecutions that we must enter the kingdom of God.' And after they had appointed elders for them in each church, with prayer and fasting they entrusted them to the Lord in whom they had come to believe.

Act 14.21–23

A reading about what a churchwarden is and does

The modern Church is based on the structure of the New Testament Church. A number of ministers are needed in each congregation. It is not satisfactory – and certainly not biblical – for the priests to assume responsibility for the entire ministry. As members of the body of Christ, we are all members of the priesthood of believers. But there are those selected by the body for specific ministries. In the Anglican Church some of these men and women comprise the church council, with two or three of the members being the churchwardens. The churchwardens function as elders in the church congregation, performing this role when they accept their high position. This ministry necessitates a relationship with Jesus Christ, a desire to please him, and openness to the Holy Spirit, so that God may be truly glorified through his Church. Out of this relationship will come a desire to share his love with others in the community and beyond. While wardens are, to some degree, members of the Church Council, they are recognized as chief among the 'elders'. This uniquely Anglican office can, and should be, an important part of building our Church.

Adapted from What is a Churchwarden? *2006 Anglican Diocese of Edmonton Canada*

Dialogue

Invite the churchwardens to come to the front of the church and ask them about their job. The congregation might ask questions, as many may not know what a churchwarden does. The churchwardens are here particularly to be thanked for the role they play in the church community. It might be suitable to present them with flowers or a gift.

Blessing	May your drainpipes be clear, may your roof keep its lead, may your responsibilities be light, may you be a person of wisdom and discernment, may you be tactful and patient, and may the blessing of God, Father, Son and Holy Spirit be upon you and all who come and go in this place, today and tomorrow. **Amen**
Songs	**As a fire is meant for burning** (*Hymns of Glory, Songs of Praise*) **Jesus calls us here to meet him** (*Iona Abbey Music Book*) **Lord, as the day begins** (*Laudate*) **Lord, for the years** (*Hymns Old and New: New Anglican Edition*) **Put peace into each other's hands** (*Hymns of Glory, Songs of Praise*) **Reign in me** (*Songs of Fellowship*)
Action	Make a cake to serve after the service. Ask everyone in the congregation to sign a card for each church-warden *(see design on page 103)*. Decorate a candle with a blessing for each churchwarden (*see How to Decorate a Candle on page 209*). Give a gift or flowers to each churchwarden on behalf of the congregation.

CARD FOR THE CHURCHWARDENS

Celebrating the Church Sitters

In an ideal world, churches would be open all the time so that anyone could come and have a quiet time of prayer or just sit and be still. It is a sad fact that many churches today are locked most of the time because of worries about security and fears that the interiors might be vandalized. One of the ways around this is to ask people to volunteer to come and open the church and sit in it so that visitors can be welcomed and see what goes on inside the building. The team of people who 'church sit' give up their time to welcome others. It is important that they are thanked for doing this.

Opening Responses

May we welcome the friend.
We welcome you.
May we welcome the stranger.
We welcome you.
May we have an open door and open hearts to always welcome.
Welcome! Amen

Thanksgiving

Heavenly Father, we give you thanks for all those who come to sit in the church so that people might be welcomed and have access when otherwise the building would be locked. We pray that we should keep the building open as much as possible, so that people do not feel they are denied access to the house of God when they need to come in. We ask that we will not fall into thinking that possessions are more important than an open door of welcome.
Amen

Readings

'Do not store up for yourselves treasures on earth, where moth and rust consume and where thieves break in and steal; but store up for yourselves treasures in heaven, where neither moth nor rust consumes and where thieves do not break in and steal. For where your treasure is, there your heart will be also.'

Matthew 6.19–21

'When the Son of Man comes in his glory, and all the angels with him, then he will sit on the throne of his glory. All the nations will be gathered before him, and he will separate people one from another as a shepherd separates the sheep from the goats, and he will put the sheep at his right hand and the goats at the left. Then the king will say to those at his right hand, "Come, you that are blessed by my Father, inherit the kingdom prepared for you from the foundation of the world; for I was hungry and you gave me food, I was thirsty and you gave me something to drink, I was a stranger and you welcomed me, I was naked and you gave me clothing, I was sick and you took care of me, I was in prison and you visited me." Then the righteous will answer him, "Lord, when was it that we saw you hungry and gave you food, or thirsty and gave you something to drink? And when was it that we saw you a stranger and welcomed you, or naked and gave you clothing? And when was it that we saw you sick or in prison and visited you?" And the king will answer them, "Truly I tell you, just as you did it to one of the least of these who are members of my family, you did it to me." Then he will say to those at his left hand, "You that are accursed, depart from me into the eternal fire prepared for the devil and his angels; for I was hungry and you gave me no food, I was thirsty and you gave me nothing to drink, I was a stranger and you did not welcome me, naked and you did not give me clothing, sick and in prison and you did not visit me." Then they also will answer, "Lord, when was it that we saw you hungry or thirsty or a stranger or naked or sick or in prison, and did not take care of you?" Then he will answer them, "Truly I tell you, just as you did not do it to one of the least of these, you did not do it to me." And these will go away into eternal punishment, but the righteous into eternal life.'

Matthew 25.31–46

Let mutual love continue. Do not neglect to show hospitality to strangers, for by doing that some have entertained angels without knowing it.

Hebrews 13.1–2

Dialogue

Invite the church sitters to come to the front. Here they might explain what church sitting entails, talk about the sort of visitors who come to the church, and how they welcome them. They might each be presented with a welcome badge to wear when they are in the church waiting to welcome people.

Blessing

May God's blessing be with you as you welcome people into this church.
May God's love be between you and each person you greet.
May you go from here blessed by your time together.
And may the blessing of God, Father, Son and Holy Spirit be upon you,
and all those you have met today and will meet tomorrow.
Amen

Songs

Come, host of heaven's high dwelling place
(*Love from Below*)

Here in this place (Gather us in)
(*Laudate*)

The King of love my shepherd is
(*Hymns Old and New: One Church, One Faith, One Lord*)

The love of God comes close
(*Iona Abbey Music Book*)

What is this place
(*Laudate*)

You are the peace of all things calm
(*Celtic Hymn Book*)

Action

Make welcome badges to be presented to each church sitter *(see design on page 107).*

BADGE FOR CHURCH SITTERS

Celebrating the Gifts of the Flower Arrangers

Many churches use flowers to make the building look more beautiful and to reflect the glory of God and the wonder of creation. Arranging flowers is a very special gift to have been given: it is not something that everyone can do. Arranging flowers can be used as an outreach into the community. Flower arrangers will often help at times of joy and times of sorrow. The work they do is important and should be celebrated by the church community. They should be thanked for using their creative gifts and for all that they do to beautify the church building.

Thanksgiving Father, we thank you for all those who week by week arrange flowers in this place. We thank you that, through their sensitivity, the church is decorated to the glory of God in times of joy and in times of sorrow. May we never take for granted the gift of time and creativity given by all in this ministry.
Amen

Bible Readings Then God said, 'Let the earth put forth vegetation: plants yielding seed, and fruit trees of every kind on earth that bear fruit with the seed in it.' And it was so. The earth brought forth vegetation: plants yielding seed of every kind, and trees of every kind bearing fruit with the seed in it. And God saw that it was good. And there was evening and there was morning, the third day.

Genesis 1.11–13

God spoke: 'Earth, green up! Grow all varieties of seed-bearing plants, every sort of fruit-bearing tree.' And there it was. Earth produced green seed-bearing plants, all varieties, and fruit-bearing trees of all sorts.

God saw that it was good. It was evening; it was morning – Day Three.

Genesis 1.11–13 (from *The Message*)

Dialogue

Ask the people who are involved in flower arranging in the church to come to the front. Ask each person to say who they are and something about what they enjoy about arranging flowers in church. At the end of the gathering, each flower arranger might be given a small bunch of flowers as a token of thanks from the church community.

Prayers
The different voices of the flower arrangers.

Voice 1	We thank you, Lord, for your wonderful creation of flowers.
Voice 2	We thank you for the people who plant the seeds that grow into the flowers.
Voice 3	We thank you for those who cut the flowers and send them to market.
Voice 4	We thank you for those who make the containers that the flowers are placed in.
Voice 5	We thank you for water that refreshes the flowers and gives them longer life in bloom.
Voice 6	We thank you that we are able to pick or buy the flowers to bring into this house of God and arrange them to God's glory.
All voices	For seeds, for growers, for markets, for flowers, **Praise God!** For glass blowers, potters, metal workers, china makers, **Praise God!** For the abundance of creativity, colours and shapes, **Praise God!** For beauty and fragrance, for flowers! **Praise God! Amen and Amen!**

Blessing	May God, who created the wonder of flowers, bless you.
	May Jesus, who came to show us God's glory in the world, bless you.
	May the Holy Spirit, who inspires us with creativity, bless you.
	May the blessing of God, Father, Son and Holy Spirit, be with you this day and always.
	Amen
Songs	**All things bright and beautiful**
	(*Hymns Old and New: New Anglican Edition*)
	I am a new creation
	(*Songs of Fellowship*)
	Living God, your word has called us
	(*New Start Hymns and Songs*)
	Lord of creation, to you be all praise!
	(*Hymns Old and New: One Church, One Faith, One Lord*)
	Take my gifts
	(*Go Before Us*)
Action	Small bunches of flowers to give to each flower arranger.

Celebrating the Intercessors

Leading intercessions in church is an important role. Finding the right words to speak when interceding between the gathered people and God is a task that needs prayerful time and consideration. It is not a gift that everyone has, and certainly not something that everyone feels able to do. So it is important that those who do agree to lead the prayers in church are encouraged and thanked.

Opening Responses
We meet as God's family gathered together to worship.
Lord, be with us.
We meet in Christ's name and offer prayers of penitence, thanksgiving and praise.
Lord, hear us.
We meet as people who respond to prayer stirred up by the Holy Spirit.
Lord, move in us.

Thanksgiving
Heavenly Father, we come to worship you Sunday by Sunday bringing our praises, hopes, fears and failings to present to you for forgiveness and blessing. We pray that all those who offer prayers in this church will be inspired to find the words which lead us to think beyond ourselves to our neighbour and out into the wider world. We pray that their words may lead us into reflection and stir us into action. We ask this in Jesus' name.
Amen

Readings
'And whenever you pray, do not be like the hypocrites; for they love to stand and pray in the synagogues and at the street corners, so that they may be seen by others. Truly I tell you, they have received their reward. But whenever you pray, go into your room and shut the door and pray to your Father who is in secret; and your Father who sees in secret will reward you.

'When you are praying, do not heap up empty phrases as the

Gentiles do; for they think that they will be heard because of their many words. Do not be like them, for your Father knows what you need before you ask him.

'Pray then in this way:

Our Father in heaven,
hallowed be your name.
Your kingdom come.
Your will be done,
on earth as it is in heaven.
Give us this day our daily bread.
And forgive us our debts,
as we also have forgiven our debtors.
And do not bring us to the time of trial,
but rescue us from the evil one.

For if you forgive others their trespasses, your heavenly Father will also forgive you; but if you do not forgive others, neither will your Father forgive your trespasses.'

Matthew 6.5–15

He was praying in a certain place, and after he had finished, one of his disciples said to him, 'Lord, teach us to pray, as John taught his disciples.' He said to them, 'When you pray, say:

Father, hallowed be your name.
Your kingdom come.
Give us each day our daily bread.
And forgive us our sins,
for we ourselves forgive everyone indebted to us.
And do not bring us to the time of trial.'

And he said to them, 'Suppose one of you has a friend, and you go to him at midnight and say to him, "Friend, lend me three loaves of bread; for a friend of mine has arrived, and I have nothing to set before him." And he answers from within, "Do not bother me; the door has already been locked, and my children are with me in bed; I cannot get up and give you anything." I tell you, even though he will not get up and give him anything because he is his friend, at least because of his persistence he will get up and give him whatever he needs.

'So I say to you, Ask, and it will be given to you; search, and you will find; knock, and the door will be opened for you. For everyone who asks receives, and everyone who searches finds, and for everyone who knocks, the door will be opened. Is there anyone among you who, if your child asks for a fish, will give a snake instead of a fish? Or if the child asks for an egg, will give a scorpion? If you then, who are evil, know how to give good gifts to your children, how much more will the heavenly Father give the Holy Spirit to those who ask him!'

Luke 11.1–13

Dialogue

Invite the people who offer the intercessions each week to come to the front. Some of them might speak about what it is like to prepare the intercessions and how they do it. The parish might buy some new books to help those who write prayers or inspire those who offer 'unwritten' prayers, and these could be shown and given to them. Each person might be given a bookmark with a prayer on it as a keepsake and a thank you.

Blessing	May your mind be filled with the wisdom, may your heart overflow with love, may the words you speak be inspired, and may you be blessed by God, the Father, Son and Holy Spirit. **Amen**

Blessing   May your mind be filled with the wisdom,
may your heart overflow with love,
may the words you speak be inspired,
and may you be blessed by God, the Father, Son and Holy Spirit.
Amen

Songs   **Be still and know that I am God**
(*Hymns Old and New: One Church, One Faith, One Lord*)

Father, I place into your hands
(*The Children's Hymnbook*)

O Lord, hear my prayer
(*Songs and Prayers from Taizé*)

Overwhelmed by love
(*The Source 3*)

Veni Sancte Spiritus (Come, Holy Spirit)
(*Songs and Prayers from Taizé*)

We walk by faith
(*Laudate*)

Action   Give each person a bookmark (*see design on page 114*).

BOOKMARK FOR INTERCESSORS

Celebrating the Mission and Outreach Groups

Why are some churches full of people on Sunday mornings and some not so well attended? It might well have something to do with the mission and outreach of the congregation. A church that looks outwards seems to attract people. Speakers invited to talk about particular charities will say that the healthiest churches they visit are the ones where the people are fully engaged with the world outside and beyond. It might be a good idea to theme a Sunday service around the church's mission and outreach involvement using the time to celebrate and update people with progress.

Opening Responses	We meet in the name of Jesus Christ. **Brothers and sisters in the family of God.** Jesus asks us to love one another. **And to love our neighbours as ourselves.**
Thanksgiving	Heavenly Father, you have called us to feed the hungry, give drink to the thirsty, welcome the stranger, clothe the naked, care for the sick and visit those in prison. We give thanks for those among us who have responded to that call and whose vision is shared with us today. Fill us with your Holy Spirit that we may all be empowered to speak out against injustice, find ways to help those who are hungry and thirsty, welcome those who are rejected, and draw near to those who are sick or imprisoned. Through Jesus Christ, our Lord. **Amen**
Readings	'When the Son of Man comes in his glory, and all the angels with him, then he will sit on the throne of his glory. All the nations will be gathered before him, and he will separate people one from another as a shepherd separates the sheep from the

goats, and he will put the sheep at his right hand and the goats at the left. Then the king will say to those at his right hand, "Come, you that are blessed by my Father, inherit the kingdom prepared for you from the foundation of the world; for I was hungry and you gave me food, I was thirsty and you gave me something to drink, I was a stranger and you welcomed me, I was naked and you gave me clothing, I was sick and you took care of me, I was in prison and you visited me." Then the righteous will answer him, "Lord, when was it that we saw you hungry and gave you food, or thirsty and gave you something to drink? And when was it that we saw you a stranger and welcomed you, or naked and gave you clothing? And when was it that we saw you sick or in prison and visited you?" And the king will answer them, "Truly I tell you, just as you did it to one of the least of these who are members of my family, you did it to me." Then he will say to those at his left hand, "You that are accursed, depart from me into the eternal fire prepared for the devil and his angels; for I was hungry and you gave me no food, I was thirsty and you gave me nothing to drink, I was a stranger and you did not welcome me, naked and you did not give me clothing, sick and in prison and you did not visit me." Then they also will answer, "Lord, when was it that we saw you hungry or thirsty or a stranger or naked or sick or in prison, and did not take care of you?" Then he will answer them, "Truly I tell you, just as you did not do it to one of the least of these, you did not do it to me." And these will go away into eternal punishment, but the righteous into eternal life.'

Matthew 25.31–46

Then Jesus, filled with the power of the Spirit, returned to Galilee, and a report about him spread through all the surrounding country. He began to teach in their synagogues and was praised by everyone.

When he came to Nazareth, where he had been brought up, he went to the synagogue on the sabbath day, as was his custom. He stood up to read, and the scroll of the prophet Isaiah was given to him. He unrolled the scroll and found the place where it was written:

'The Spirit of the Lord is upon me,
because he has anointed me
to bring good news to the poor.
He has sent me to proclaim release to the captives
and recovery of sight to the blind,
to let the oppressed go free,
to proclaim the year of the Lord's favour.'
And he rolled up the scroll, gave it back to the attendant, and
sat down. The eyes of all in the synagogue were fixed on him.
Then he began to say to them, 'Today this scripture has been
fulfilled in your hearing.'

Luke 4.14–21

All who believed were together and had all things in common;
they would sell their possessions and goods and distribute the
proceeds to all, as any had need. Day by day, as they spent
much time together in the temple, they broke bread at home
and ate their food with glad and generous hearts, praising God
and having the goodwill of all the people. And day by day the
Lord added to their number those who were being saved.

Acts 2.44–47

Now the whole group of those who believed were of one heart
and soul, and no one claimed private ownership of any possessions, but everything they owned was held in common. With
great power the apostles gave their testimony to the resurrection of the Lord Jesus, and great grace was upon them all.
There was not a needy person among them, for as many as
owned lands or houses sold them and brought the proceeds
of what was sold. They laid it at the apostles' feet, and it was
distributed to each as any had need.

Acts 4.32–35

Dialogue

Invite representatives of the different outreach groups to the front and allow each one to speak for a few minutes on their particular situation, illustrating their words with a PowerPoint presentation. If there are more than two speakers, there might be a song in the middle. At the end, all those who have come forward face the congregation to receive the following blessing.

Blessing	May those who hunger and thirst, **Receive God's blessing.** May those whom the world rejects, **Receive God's blessing.** May those who live in poverty, **Receive God's blessing.** May those who are sick, **Receive God's blessing.** May those who are imprisoned, **Receive God's blessing.** And may you, who have answered the call to tend the broken body of Christ in the world, **Receive God's blessing now and always.** **Amen**
	OR
	Jesus says, 'Just as you do it to the least of these who are members of my family, you do it to me.' May you, who have answered the call to tend the broken body of Christ in the world, **Receive God's blessing now and always.** **Amen**
Songs	**Alleluia! Raise the Gospel** (*Go Before Us*) **Blest are they, the poor in spirit** (*Hymns of Glory, Songs of Praise*) **Christ has no hands but ours** *Sheet Music (See section on Hymns and Songs)*

Filled with compassion (For all the people who live on the earth)
(*The Source 3*)

Send down the fire
(*Cantate*)

We will take what you offer
(*There Is One Among Us*)

Action

Ask for representatives of the different groups to prepare a short update of their work – possibly illustrated by a Power-Point presentation.

If there isn't one already, make up a display board with photos and information – this can be kept up to date and placed where everyone can see it.

Run a PowerPoint display of photos for people to look at over coffee.

Give people leaflets about the different supported projects – either official ones or home-made ones.

After the service, invite people to an informal meal and serve food from the countries supported.

Have a table at coffee time selling fairly traded goods and giving information about Fair Trade.

Celebrating the Parish Magazine Production Team

A parish magazine is a living and changing picture of life and activity in the church. It gives contact information for key people and a diary of forthcoming services and events. It marks the seasons with articles, news items, reports, stories and poetry, and much else. It is often read by a much wider audience – people who live in the neighbourhood but who may not necessarily attend the church. It may be their only connection with the local church. It is also a permanent record of baptisms, weddings and funerals that have taken place. It is, by its very nature, a witness to the worshipping community in that place. Invite all those involved with producing the parish magazine to the service. Remember not only the editor but the designers, illustrators, typesetters, proof readers, printers, collators and deliverers, and others involved in any way with producing the magazine.

Thanksgiving Father, we give thanks for our parish magazine production team. We thank you for the skills of the editor, *N*, and for all those who work together to produce our magazine month by month. May all who are involved – designers, illustrators, typesetters, proof readers, printers, collators and deliverers – know that they are valued and appreciated. We give thanks, too, for the creativity of all those who contribute articles and stories to the magazine and who, by doing so, make it a living account of the life and mission of this church community season by season.
Amen

Readings They devoted themselves to the apostles' teaching and fellowship, to the breaking of bread and the prayers.

Awe came upon everyone, because many wonders and signs were being done by the apostles. All who believed were together and had all things in common; they would sell their possessions and goods and distribute the proceeds to all, as any had need. Day by day, as they spent much time together in the temple, they broke bread at home and ate their food with glad and generous hearts, praising God and having the goodwill of all the people. And day by day the Lord added to their number those who were being saved.

Acts 2.42–47

The end of all things is near; therefore be serious and discipline yourselves for the sake of your prayers. Above all, maintain constant love for one another, for love covers a multitude of sins. Be hospitable to one another without complaining. Like good stewards of the manifold grace of God, serve one another with whatever gift each of you has received. Whoever speaks must do so as one speaking the very words of God; whoever serves must do so with the strength that God supplies, so that God may be glorified in all things through Jesus Christ. To him belong the glory and the power for ever and ever. Amen.

1 Peter 4.7–11

Dialogue

Invite the current magazine editor and any previous editors to the front of the church and ask them about their job. A parish magazine's appearance and regular content may have evolved and changed over time. It might be fun to hold up a copy of a magazine from former times alongside a current one. An editor is often looking for new contributors to the magazine and this might be a moment to say something about that, too. Present the current editor with a gift connected to the job.

Blessing   May the blessing of God be in our thinking.
                     Lord, bless our thoughts with wisdom.
                     May the blessing of Jesus be in our speaking.
                     Lord, bless our words with kindness.
                     May the blessing of the Holy Spirit be in our doing.
                     Lord, bless our actions with love.
                     Amen

Songs

Christ beside us
(*Go Before Us*)

Community of Christ
(*Go Before Us*)

Jesus put this song into our hearts
(*Hymns Old and New: New Anglican Edition*)

Let us build a house (All are welcome)
(*Laudate*)

Sisters and brothers, with one voice
(*Iona Abbey Music Book*)

The Church is wherever God's people are praising
(*Hymns of Glory, Songs of Praise*)

Action

Give the editor a CD of clip-art to use in the magazine or a resource book of poems and reflections.

Celebrating the Parish Secretary and Office Team

The parish secretary in any parish has a vital role to play, and this should sometimes be acknowledged and celebrated. Very often the first port of call for a newcomer, possibly enquiring about a wedding, baptism or funeral, is the parish office. The secretary, or whoever responds, has an important pastoral role to play – whether this is a face-to-face encounter, on the telephone or by email. Also, the parish office team may, week after week, look after the paperwork, photocopying and pew-sheets. If there are parish rooms, it is the office team who will most likely look after the bookings and make sure that things are running smoothly. The parish secretary and team also work closely with the clergy and ministry team.

Thanksgiving Heavenly Father, we give you thanks for N *(and for all the office team)* working in the parish office. The smooth running of this church relies on N's calm and efficient manner. Whether dealing with a baptism or wedding enquiry, or speaking with someone newly bereaved, or taking a booking for the church hall, this is a pastoral role and is valued by us all. May N continue to keep us all in calm order, patiently answering our queries and sorting out the day-to-day tasks *he/she* undertakes on our behalf and to the glory of God.
Amen

Readings Now you are the body of Christ and individually members of it. And God has appointed in the church first apostles, second prophets, third teachers; then deeds of power, then gifts of healing, forms of assistance, forms of leadership, various kinds of tongues. Are all apostles? Are all prophets? Are all teachers? Do all work miracles? Do all possess gifts of healing? Do all speak in tongues? Do all interpret? But strive for the greater gifts. And I will show you a still more excellent way.

1 Corinthians 12.27–31

As God's chosen ones, holy and beloved, clothe yourselves with compassion, kindness, humility, meekness, and patience. Bear with one another and, if anyone has a complaint against another, forgive each other; just as the Lord has forgiven you, so you also must forgive. Above all, clothe yourselves with love, which binds everything together in perfect harmony. And let the peace of Christ rule in your hearts, to which indeed you were called in the one body. And be thankful. Let the word of Christ dwell in you richly; teach and admonish one another in all wisdom; and with gratitude in your hearts sing psalms, hymns, and spiritual songs to God. And whatever you do, in word or deed, do everything in the name of the Lord Jesus, giving thanks to God the Father through him.

Colossians 3.12–17

Dialogue

Invite the parish secretary and office team to come forward. This is a good time to remind people about when the office is open and how the team can help with all sorts of things. Present a gift to the team and give them a blessing

Blessing   May God, who calls each one of us to do his work,
bless and keep you.
May Jesus, whose way of life leads to all truth,
bless and keep you.
May the Holy Spirit, who dances through our days,
weaving the patterns of life,
bless and keep you now and always.
Amen

Songs   **Be thou my vision**
(*Hymns Old and New: New Anglican Edition*)

Everyday God
(*Restless Is the Heart*)

Forth in your name, O Lord, I go
(*Sing Glory*)

Go peaceful, in gentleness
(*Hymns Old and New: One Church, One Faith, One Lord*)

Litany and Prayers (Holden Evening Prayer)
(*Cantate*)

Spirit, breathe on us
(*Songs of Fellowship*)

Action   Ask the parish secretary and office team to choose a favourite hymn or song for the service.

Present the office team with a gift (new mugs or a cafetière).

Present the office team with a token for a meal in a local restaurant.

Celebrating the Parochial Church Council

The Parochial Church Council (PCC) is a body of lay people elected at the Annual Parochial Church Meeting who work with the incumbent and other clergy in the parish, churchwardens and readers, and other ex-officio and co-opted members. The Council is responsible for the initiation, conduct and development of the church's work within the parish and beyond. Serving on the PCC is an important role and can be a very rewarding one. Members of the PCC should be known by the congregation so that people know who to talk to when they want something discussed at a PCC meeting.

Thanksgiving   Heavenly Father, we give you thanks and praise that you call us to do your work here in this place. We give special thanks today for those who serve on the Parochial Church Council. Theirs is an important role as they discuss the day-to-day running of the parish so that we, as brothers and sisters in Christ, may best witness to your kingdom. Fill them with your Holy Spirit and give them patience and understanding as they listen to each other, and the grace to make wise decisions underpinned and guided by your truth.
Amen

Readings   To you, O LORD, I lift up my soul.
O my God, in you I trust;
do not let me be put to shame;
do not let my enemies exult over me.
Do not let those who wait for you be put to shame;
let them be ashamed who are wantonly treacherous.

Make me to know your ways, O LORD;
teach me your paths.
Lead me in your truth, and teach me,

for you are the God of my salvation;
for you I wait all day long.

Be mindful of your mercy, O LORD, and of your steadfast
love,
for they have been from of old.
Do not remember the sins of my youth or my transgressions;
according to your steadfast love remember me,
for your goodness' sake, O LORD!

Good and upright is the LORD;
therefore he instructs sinners in the way.
He leads the humble in what is right,
and teaches the humble his way.
All the paths of the Lord are steadfast love and faithfulness,
for those who keep his covenant and his decrees.

Psalm 25.1–10

Grace to you and peace from God our Father and the Lord
Jesus Christ.
   I give thanks to my God always for you because of the grace
of God that has been given you in Christ Jesus, for in every way
you have been enriched in him, in speech and knowledge of
every kind – just as the testimony of Christ has been strengthened among you – so that you are not lacking in any spiritual
gift as you wait for the revealing of our Lord Jesus Christ. He
will also strengthen you to the end, so that you may be blame-
less on the day of our Lord Jesus Christ. God is faithful; by him
you were called into the fellowship of his Son, Jesus Christ our
Lord.
   Now I appeal to you, brothers and sisters, by the name of
our Lord Jesus Christ, that all of you should be in agreement
and that there should be no divisions among you, but that you
should be united in the same mind and the same purpose.

1 Corinthians 1.3–10

Finally, all of you, have unity of spirit, sympathy, love for one
another, a tender heart, and a humble mind. Do not repay evil

for evil or abuse for abuse; but, on the contrary, repay with a blessing. It is for this that you were called – that you might inherit a blessing. For

'Those who desire life
and desire to see good days,
let them keep their tongues from evil
and their lips from speaking deceit;
let them turn away from evil and do good;
let them seek peace and pursue it.
For the eyes of the Lord are on the righteous,
and his ears are open to their prayer.
But the face of the Lord is against those who do evil.'

1 Peter 3.8–12

Dialogue

Ask all current members of the PCC to come forward. Ask one or two people about being on the PCC – who can join, how long the commitment is for, how often the Council meets, etc. Then it might be fun to ask anyone else in the congregation who has served on the PCC to stand up where they are. In a healthy church there will be many who have spent time serving on the PCC – but sometimes it can be the same people over and over again!

Blessing   May God the Father fill you with all wisdom,
may God the Son surround you with love,
may God the Holy Spirit breathe in you and give you life,
and may the blessing of the Three be with you always.
Amen

Songs   **A new commandment**
(*Hymns Old and New: One Church, One Faith, One Lord*)

Christ is made the sure foundation
(*Sing Glory*)

Father in heaven, how we love you (Blessed be the Lord God Almighty)
(*The Source 3*)

Gifts of the Spirit (When our Lord walked the earth)
(*Iona Abbey Music Book*)

Let us build a house (All are welcome)
(*Laudate*)

Living God, your word has called us
(*New Start Hymns and Songs*)

Action   Give name badges to each member of the PCC.

Display a photo of each member on a wall.

Have a celebration after the service.

Plan a PCC meal in a local restaurant.

Plan a PCC Away-Day for quiet time and fellowship.

Celebrating the Servers

It is the tradition in some churches to have a faithful band of servers who Sunday by Sunday serve at the altar. There might just be one or there might be several. It is important that this work in the church is acknowledged and at least once a year the work of the servers might be celebrated. The servers for the day may already be up by the altar so they and any others who are in the congregation that Sunday should be invited to come and stand together in front of the people. Some churches have medallions or crosses for the servers to wear; these may be given out after a probationary period. This would be an excellent time to make these presentations. If this is not the case it might be that the church family could give the servers a small gift in thanks for the work they do.

Prayers   *Each prayer might be said by a different voice*

We ask God's blessing on all those who carry the processional cross *(the crucifer)*. May they have strong, steady arms as they lift the cross up high. As it is carried around, between and among the people in the church, may it be seen by all as a symbol of Christ's forgiving love.
Amen

We ask for God's blessing on all those who carry candles *(the acolytes)*. We ask that, as they hold the candles up to illuminate the word of God, all darkness will be dispelled and those who hear God's word will be filled with God's light.
Amen

We ask for God's blessing on all those who carry the incense *(in a thurible, the thurifers)*. We ask that, as the smoke rises up to the rafters, so may our prayers be lifted up to God. And as the altar, and we, are censed, we pray that we should all be worthy to be called the body of Christ.
Amen

Cross-carriers, light-holders, incense-bearers, we thank you for all you do in this church Sunday by Sunday.

Amen. Praise God! Alleluia!

Songs

Be still, for the presence of the Lord
(*Hymns Old and New: One Church, One Faith, One Lord*)

Brother, sister, let me serve you
(*Hymns Old and New: One Church, One Faith, One Lord*)

From heaven you came (The Servant King)
(*The Source 3*)

Here in this place (Gather us in)
(*Laudate*)

Lift high the Cross
(*Hymns Old and New: New Anglican Edition*)

Longing for light (Christ, be our light)
(*Christ, Be Our Light*)

Celebrating the Sidespeople

In most churches, every Sunday a group of people take it in turns to be sides-people. They often welcome people at the door, hand out the hymn books and generally help to make the service run smoothly. This is an important part of the serving community of the church, and every so often the sidespeople should be thanked for what they do.

Thanksgiving We pause at the end of this service to give thanks for all those who Sunday by Sunday act as sidespeople. We pray that they will do this job with joy and enthusiasm, and that the order they bring to the service will enable the congregation to worship and glorify our Lord.
Amen

Dialogue

Ask all the current sidespeople to come to the front. Ask one or two to give a brief description of what the job entails, what the commitment is, and what they particularly enjoy about it. Present each person with a card, and give them the following blessing.

Blessing May you welcome the stranger at the door,
may you serve the church community with joy,
may you provide a calm order to the service,
may you all be blessed by doing this work,
and may the blessing of God, Father, Son and Holy Spirit,
be upon all who are gathered here today.
Amen

OR

May you . . .
  welcome with love,
  serve with joy,
  and go out in peace to continue to love and serve the Lord.
Amen

Action

Give each sidesperson a name badge saying who they are and what they do.

Take a photo of each sidesperson which can be put on a board with their name underneath so that everyone can identify them.

Give each sidesperson a thank-you card signed by the vicar and churchwardens *(see design on page 134)*.

THANK-YOU CARD FOR SIDESPERSON

Celebrating the Social and Fellowship Group

Many churches today have social events at the heart of their outreach, whether it is making coffee or tea after the service on Sunday or, for example, providing lunch at an annual Patronal Festival. Whenever a social event happens there will be a group of people who organize the invitations, make the drinks and bake the cakes. This is a very time-consuming activity and is usually offered with much joy, and sometimes with little thanks. It is important that these people are thanked for what they do.

Opening Responses	Jesus took bread and broke it and shared it with those at the table with him. **Thank you, Lord, for your gift of kindness.** Jesus took loaves and fishes, blessed them and fed all at the gathering. **Thank you, Lord, for your gift of generosity.** Jesus turned water into wine so the wedding would be full of joy. **Thank you, Lord, for your gift of hospitality.**
Thanksgiving	Heavenly Father, we thank you for all those who spend time serving people in this church with food and drink. We thank you for their gifts in baking and food preparation. We thank you for their generosity with time and money. We thank you that they understand how important it is to serve one another and that in so doing they are reaching out to their neighbour by offering hospitality. Praise God! **Amen**
Readings	While they were eating, Jesus took a loaf of bread, and after blessing it he broke it, gave it to the disciples, and said, 'Take, eat; this is my body.' Then he took a cup, and after giving

thanks he gave it to them, saying, 'Drink from it, all of you; for this is my blood of the covenant, which is poured out for many for the forgiveness of sins.'

Matthew 26.26–28

When he went ashore, he saw a great crowd; and he had compassion for them and cured their sick. When it was evening, the disciples came to him and said, 'This is a deserted place, and the hour is now late; send the crowds away so that they may go into the villages and buy food for themselves.' Jesus said to them, 'They need not go away; you give them something to eat.' They replied, 'We have nothing here but five loaves and two fish.' And he said, 'Bring them here to me.' Then he ordered the crowds to sit down on the grass. Taking the five loaves and the two fish, he looked up to heaven, and blessed and broke the loaves, and gave them to the disciples, and the disciples gave them to the crowds. And all ate and were filled; and they took up what was left over of the broken pieces, twelve baskets full. And those who ate were about five thousand men, besides women and children.

Matthew 14.14–21

Dialogue

Invite those who are on the coffee rota and those who are in the fellowship or social group to come to the front of the church. This is an opportunity for the church congregation to show their appreciation for all that these people do in service to others. Each one might be given a card, and also a helium-filled balloon as a sign of the fun and pleasure that they give others through their cooking and serving.

Blessing   May God, the bringer of love, bless you,
may Jesus, who shares bread with all, bless you,
and may the Holy Spirit, who brings celebration and joy, bless you.

OR

When cake is cut and shared, God is there.
When coffee and tea are poured, God is there.
When washing-up is done, God is there.
God of cake,
God of coffee and tea,
God of washing-up,
Bless those who offer their gifts of hospitality in this church.
And may the blessing of God, Father, Son and Holy Spirit, be
upon you all, today and always.
Amen

Songs

Brother, sister let me serve you
(*Hymns Old and New: One Church, One Faith, One Lord*)

Jesus calls us here to meet him
(*Iona Abbey Music Book*)

Let there be love
(*Hymns Old and New: New Anglican Edition*)

Take my gifts
(*Go Before Us*)

Thanks be to God
(*Laudate*)

When I needed a neighbour
(*Hymns of Glory, Songs of Praise*)

Action

Print and sign cards *(see design on page 138).*

Give out helium-filled balloons.

A CARD FOR SOCIAL AND FELLOWSHIP GROUP

PRAISE GOD FOR COFFEE TEA and CAKES

Celebrating the Treasurer and Stewardship Team

Being the treasurer in a parish is a vitally important role and one that is sacrificial in terms of time spent and responsibility felt. Reporting regularly to the PCC, the treasurer must keep a record of monies raised by the congregation in different ways and then spent on their behalf for the church and its outreach. Among other things, the treasurer is also responsible for administering the different funds held by the parish and has to produce a financial report at the Annual Parochial Church Meeting. The stewardship team acknowledges that all things come from God and that we all have a responsibility to care for what God has given – the team encourages the people to offer their time and different gifts, or to contribute financially as best they are able.

Thanksgiving   Lord, we give you thanks and praise that you shower us with abundant blessings. We know that all things come from you and that all we give of ourselves is yours in the first place. Each one of us has a part to play as a member of your body, the Church. We thank you for our treasurer and for our stewardship team. With their careful administration of the church's finance, along with gentle encouragement to explore and use the gifts we all have to offer, the Holy Spirit can move and work in this place among your people to your glory.
Amen

Readings   Set apart a tithe of all the yield of your seed that is brought in yearly from the field. In the presence of the Lord your God, in the place that he will choose as a dwelling for his name, you shall eat the tithe of your grain, your wine, and your oil, as well as the firstlings of your herd and flock, so that you may learn to fear the LORD your God always.

Deuteronomy 14.22–23

For you know the generous act of our Lord Jesus Christ, that though he was rich, yet for your sakes he became poor, so that by his poverty you might become rich. And in this matter I am giving my advice: it is appropriate for you who began last year not only to do something but even to desire to do something – now finish doing it, so that your eagerness may be matched by completing it according to your means. For if the eagerness is there, the gift is acceptable according to what one has – not according to what one does not have. I do not mean that there should be relief for others and pressure on you, but it is a question of a fair balance between your present abundance and their need, so that their abundance may be for your need, in order that there may be a fair balance. As it is written,

> 'The one who had much did not have too much,
> and the one who had little did not have too little.'

2 Corinthians 8.9–15

The point is this: the one who sows sparingly will also reap sparingly, and the one who sows bountifully will also reap bountifully. Each of you must give as you have made up your mind, not reluctantly or under compulsion, for God loves a cheerful giver. And God is able to provide you with every blessing in abundance, so that by always having enough of everything, you may share abundantly in every good work. As it is written,

> 'He scatters abroad, he gives to the poor;
> his righteousness endures for ever.'

He who supplies seed to the sower and bread for food will supply and multiply your seed for sowing and increase the harvest of your righteousness. You will be enriched in every way for your great generosity, which will produce thanksgiving to God through us; for the rendering of this ministry not only supplies the needs of the saints but also overflows with many thanksgivings to God. Through the testing of this ministry you glorify God by your obedience to the confession of the gospel of Christ and by the generosity of your sharing with them and with all others, while they long for you and pray for you because of the surpassing grace of God that he has given you. Thanks be to God for his indescribable gift!

2 Corinthians 9.6–15

Dialogue

Invite the treasurer and stewardship team to the front of the church. This is not the time for questions and answers but it might be an opportunity to acknowledge and give thanks for all the different activities in the church and encourage people to think about what they might be able to offer in terms of 'time and talents' that they may not have thought about. Thanks can be given to the treasurer and stewardship team for their work, followed by a round of applause! (These are not the easiest of jobs to take on.)

Blessing	May God the Father, who has given us all things, bless us, may God the Son, who entrusts his Church to us, bless us, may the God the Holy Spirit, whose power fills us with creative energy, bless us, may these Three; Father, Son and Holy Spirit, bless us and keep us, this day and always. **Amen**
Songs	**Beauty for brokenness (God of the poor)** (*The Source 3*)
	Christian people, sing together (*New Start Hymns and Songs*)
	God in such love for us lent us this planet (*Hymns of Glory, Songs of Praise*)
	Jubilee Song (*Restless Is the Heart*)
	We are many parts (*Laudate*)
	When God Almighty came to earth (God on earth) (*Hymns Old and New: New Anglican Edition*)
Action	This might be an opportunity to list (or show), either on a piece of paper that can be given out, or as a PowerPoint display at the beginning or end of the service, all the different activities that church members are involved in.
	These resources might be used at a service that forms the start or finish of a stewardship campaign where the team actively talk to people to encourage them to use their gifts for the benefit of all.

Celebrating the Webmaster (and IT Team)

It is only relatively recently that internet websites have become a part of the daily life for many of us – and now increasingly parish churches have designed their own. Information about a particular parish church can, through a website, be viewed from anywhere in the world that has an internet connection. Some parish churches include Sunday sermons on their websites. This obviously gives churches a huge opportunity to inform people about their teaching, life and mission. With a few clicks of the mouse, someone on the other side of the world can visit, in cyber terms, a church thousands of miles away.

Thanksgiving   Lord, we praise you for the wonders of information technology. In today's world of instant communication, first impressions are vitally important. We give thanks for the work of *N*, our webmaster (*and for his/her supporting team*). Through *his/her* careful design, our website welcomes and informs, giving visitors a clear and up-to-date picture of our parish. For those who are already a part of our church, the website provides a living diary and a source of information. We pray that those who visit the site for the first time will find something in it of God's love and grace, and that those who are searching may be encouraged further to seek us out so that we may welcome them.
Amen

Readings   O Lᴏʀᴅ, our Sovereign,
how majestic is your name in all the earth!
You have set your glory above the heavens.
Out of the mouths of babes and infants
you have founded a bulwark because of your foes,
to silence the enemy and the avenger.
When I look at your heavens, the work of your fingers,

the moon and the stars that you have established;
what are human beings that you are mindful of them,
mortals that you care for them?
Yet you have made them a little lower than God,
and crowned them with glory and honour.
You have given them dominion over the works of your hands;
you have put all things under their feet,
all sheep and oxen,
and also the beasts of the field,
the birds of the air, and the fish of the sea,
whatever passes along the paths of the seas.
O LORD, our Sovereign,
how majestic is your name in all the earth!

Psalm 8

Now there are varieties of gifts, but the same Spirit; and
there are varieties of services, but the same Lord; and there
are varieties of activities, but it is the same God who activates
all of them in everyone. To each is given the manifestation of
the Spirit for the common good. To one is given through the
Spirit the utterance of wisdom, and to another the utterance
of knowledge according to the same Spirit, to another faith by
the same Spirit, to another gifts of healing by the one Spirit,
to another the working of miracles, to another prophecy, to
another the discernment of spirits, to another various kinds of
tongues, to another the interpretation of tongues. All these are
activated by one and the same Spirit, who allots to each one
individually just as the Spirit chooses.

1 Corinthians 12.4–11

Dialogue

*Invite the webmaster (and his/her team) to come to the front and ask them to
talk a little about maintaining the parish website. Present them with a box of Fair
Trade chocolates.*

Prayer

For the wonders of information technology,
We praise you, Lord.

For the internet and the opportunities it offers,
We praise you, Lord.

For humankind's ability to learn new skills,
We praise you, Lord.

For the wisdom to use knowledge wisely,
We ask you, Lord.

For the chance to spread the Good News of Jesus,
We thank you, Lord.

For all who seek to know your love, and joy, and peace,
We pray to you, Lord.

For all your people, that we may learn to follow you in faith,
We pray to you, Lord, and give you thanks and praise.
Amen

Songs

Christ be beside me
(*Celtic Hymn Book*)

For I'm building a people of power
(*Hymns Old and New: One Church, One Faith, One Lord*)

Halle, halle, hallelujah! (O God, to whom shall we go?)
(*Hymns of Glory, Songs of Praise*)

O God, you search me
(*Christ, Be Our light*)

Send out your light
(*Come All You People*)

You are the vine
(*Songs of Fellowship*)

Action

Place photos of the webmaster and IT team on a wall so that everyone can identify them.

Buy a large box of Fair Trade chocolates.

Farewell to a Gap Year Student Going Travelling

Ask the student to come to the front. Introduce the student and ask about his/her plans for the gap year – where they plan to go, how they will get there, who they will travel with, what they will do, when they will leave, and when they plan to return.

Prayer Father, we place N into your loving care. Be *his/her* constant guide and companion. In times of stress, bring calm. In times of loneliness, bring friends. In times of fellowship, bring joy. We pray that *he/she* will carry your love wherever *he/she* goes and shine as a light in your wonderful world.
Amen

Information leaflet

Before the service, find out where the gap year student will be travelling to. Ask someone in the congregation to spend some time putting together an information leaflet to give to the traveller. Here are some ideas to include:

- *The website address for GapAid <www.gapaid.org> This is a website specifically designed to support gap year travellers while they travel.*
- *Some information about the church, and maybe a photo, so if they meet fellow Christians on their journey they can show them where they worship.*
- *Information about churches and times of services in some of the cities they are going to.*
- *Emergency phone numbers of useful contacts in any of the countries being visited. This might include Embassies and High Commissions.*
- *Other phone numbers or email addresses – ask the congregation if they have friends or family in the countries to be visited and if they would be happy to supply contact numbers or addresses.*
- *A prayer on a card to be said at the beginning of a new day, 'Father, wrap your loving and protecting arms around me today as I venture out into the unknown. Amen.'*

- *A worldwide phone card.*
- *A pocket cross.*

Blessing

May your rucksack be light,
may your pathway be smooth,
may your adventure be enriching,
may you give as well as receive,
and may you return safely home at your journey's end.
Amen

OR

May God bless you as you travel out from here
on your new adventure.
Amen
May God's love be between you and all whom you meet.
Amen
Go in the light and love of the Lord.
Amen

And the blessing . . .

Songs

As the final hymn in the service sing one of the following:

Do not be afraid
(*Hymns Old and New: New Anglican Edition*)

Faithful One
(*Sing Glory*)

One more step along the road we go
(*Hymns Old and New: New Anglican Edition*)

Teach me to dance
(*Hymns Old and New: One Church, One Faith, One Lord*)

The Lord's my shepherd (Townend)
(*Sing Glory*)

You shall go out with joy
(*Hymns Old and New: New Anglican Edition*)

Action

Make a leaflet to give to the student.

Print card and ask everyone to sign *(see design on page 147)*.

CARD FOR GAP YEAR STUDENT

FATHER WRAP YOUR LOVING & PROTECTING ARMS AROUND ME TODAY AS I VENTURE OUT INTO THE UNKNOWN. AMEN

Farewell to a Group Going on Pilgrimage

Ask one of the organizers of the parish pilgrimage to come forward. Let the person speak to the congregation a little about the place of pilgrimage and what the people on the journey will be doing.

Prayer

For pilgrims and sacred journeys,
We thank you, O Lord.
For saints who have gone before,
We thank you, O Lord.
For time spent together but also apart,
We thank you, O Lord.

In stories retold and relived,
Be with us, O Lord.
In seeking the 'thin' place,
Be with us, O Lord.
In letting go and letting be,
Be with us, O Lord.

For bread broken and shared,
We thank you, O Lord.
For laughter and fellowship,
We thank you, O Lord.
For rest and refreshment,
We thank you, O Lord.
Amen

Blessing

May you be kept safe by God on your journey,
may you meet with Jesus along the way,
may you be filled with the peace and joy of the Holy Spirit,
and may you be richly blessed on your pilgrimage.
Amen

Songs

Be thou my vision
(*Hymns Old and New: New Anglican Edition*)

Christ be beside me
(*Celtic Hymn Book*)

Lead me, Lord
(*Sing Glory*)

May the peace of the Lord Christ go with you
(*Celtic Hymn Book*)

One more step along the world I go
(*Hymns Old and New: New Anglican Edition*)

Walk with me, O my Lord
(*Liturgical Hymns Old and New*)

Action

Give each pilgrim a small journal to take with them.

Give each pilgrim a small cross or pilgrim's prayer card to carry in their pocket.

Take a photograph of the group as they set off, to display on the notice board.

On their return ask a member of the pilgrim party to give an illustrated talk about the pilgrimage.

Farewell to a Significant Lay Person Leaving the Parish

Ask the person leaving to come to the front. If they are well-known as a member of the congregation there will be no need to introduce them, but not everyone may know where they are going and what they will be doing, so ask them to speak for a few moments about their future plans.

Prayer	Father, we pray for N as *he/she* sets out on the next part of *his/her* life adventure. As N leaves us here with so many good memories, we pray that *his/her* new church will welcome *him/her* and that *he/she* will quickly become part of a new church family.
	Amen

Present the person leaving with one, or some, of the following.

Book of Memories

In the weeks before their last Sunday, put together a Book of Memories for the person who is leaving. Ask members of the congregation to give photos or written stories about events that the person has been involved in over their time in the congregation.

Farewell card

In the Sundays leading up to the person's departure, ask everyone to sign a farewell card.

Gift

In the Sundays leading up to the person's departure, make a collection so a gift may be bought. Think carefully about what the person might like. It might be a voucher for a hobby (gardening, book, theatre), or there may be something they would like for their new home.

Guide Books or Maps

Find out where the person is moving to and make a gift of some guide books or maps of the new area.

Blessing	*N*, we praise God and give thanks for all the many blessings we have shared together.
	As you leave this place and go on your new adventure, may you be aware of God's presence with you wherever you go.
	May you be made welcome in your new home, and by your new church family.
	We say farewell with a heavy heart, but we know you will take your many gifts to your new home and continue to shine as a light in God's wonderful world.
	And may the blessing of God almighty, the Father, the Son, and the Holy Spirit, be with you today and always. **Amen**
Action	Put together the gifts for the person.
	Ask everyone to sign a card *(see design on page 152)*.

CARD FOR LAY PERSON LEAVING PARISH

AS YOU GO FROM HERE CONTINUE TO SHINE AS A LIGHT IN GOD'S WONDERFUL WORLD

Farewell to a Student Departing for University

Ask the student to come to the front. Introduce the student and ask him/her about the university and what they will be studying.

Prayer   Father, we pray for N as *he/she* sets out on the next part of *his/her* journey. Give *him/her* courage and strength as *he/she* leaves home and faces the first days and weeks at university. Give *him/her* new friends and companions who can share *his/her* journey with all its ups and downs, and walk with *him/her* as *he/she* learns and grows and becomes more fully the person *he/she* is destined to be. And bring *him/her* back home again full of stories to tell and adventures to share.
Amen

Bag for Life

N is presented with a Bag for Life. Members of the congregation come forward, each holding something that might be useful for university. Items may include chocolate, train and bus timetables for visits home, a phone card, a list of phone numbers, a students' recipe book or a collection of recipes from the church congregation, a group photo of church friends, a signed card, a Bible, a prayer book, a small cross, a candle. Each item is presented to N and placed in the Bag for Life with appropriate words:

> Here is emergency chocolate.
> Here are bus and train timetables.
> Here is a phone card to help you to keep in touch.
> Here are the phone numbers of lots of friends.
> Here are simple recipes to try out.
> Here is a photo to remind you of your friends here.
> Here is a card signed by us all wishing you well.

Here is a Bible to guide your way.
Here is a prayer book to dip into when you need.
Here is a cross to carry in your pocket.
Here is a candle to light your path.

Blessing

Invite friends of N to come forward and surround N. They may like to lay their hands on N.

N, as you leave this place and go to university,
may God go with you.

As you learn and grow,
may Jesus be close to you.

As you explore and are challenged,
may the Holy Spirit protect and guide you.

And may the blessing of God almighty,
the Father, the Son, and the Holy Spirit,
be with you today and always.
Amen

Action

Make and fill a Bag for Life *(see How to Make on page 207)* and stock up on appropriate contents.

Ask everyone to sign a card *(see design on page 155)*.

CARD FOR STUDENT LEAVING FOR UNIVERSITY

AS YOU LEAVE THIS PLACE
& GO TO UNIVERSITY
MAY GOD GO WITH YOU
AS YOU LEARN & GROW

MAY JESUS BE CLOSE TO YOU
AS YOU EXPLORE
and are
CHALLENGED

MAY THE HOLY SPIRIT
PROTECT & GUIDE YOU
& MAY GOD'S BLESSING
BE UPON YOU
TODAY & ALWAYS

Farewell to an Ordinand Starting Training

Ask the ordinand to come to the front with his/her family – wife/husband, children or parents. Introduce the ordinand and the family and ask him/her to tell the congregation about his/her plans for theological college or the course he/she will be taking. He/she might say something about where he/she will be going and what he/she expects to be doing. Remember that the whole family will be involved, so also ask to hear what the husband/wife will be doing and, if there are children, include them as well. Where will they live? Where will they go to school? Acknowledge that this is a great and special occasion for the congregation. To have someone go out from a church community to be trained for ordination is a wonderful event to be celebrated.

Prayer   Father, we thank you for N's calling to the ordained ministry.
                    We thank you for the time *he/she* has spent with this congregation.
                    We thank you for the many blessings *he/she* has given to us.
                    And now as *he/she (and the family)* goes from here, we pray that *he/she (they)* will know that *he/she(they)* journeys with our love, prayers and support.
                    Amen

A Gift

There is now an opportunity for the congregation to give a small gift to the ordinand to mark his/her going to training college. This needs to be thought about carefully and be relevant to the person. Below are some ideas, though it might well be that there is something obvious that comes to mind. If there is a partner or children involved in the move, do make sure that he/she is included in the gift giving. Having a partner or parent who goes to college affects the whole family and often involves change or even sacrifice on everyone's part, and it is right that that should be acknowledged. Here are some ideas:

- An album put together by the congregation. Everyone in the congregation might be asked to supply a photo of themselves and write about some event that they have shared with the ordinand.
- Supermarket vouchers. If the ordinand will be moving house to go to college, find out the name of the local supermarket and buy some vouchers suggesting that *he/she* (and the family) might like to buy a few pre-prepared meals when they first move.
- A gift for the house or to help with studying. If the congregation has had a collection to buy a present, find out if there is anything that the ordinand would like for their new home or to help with studying.
- Maps or guide books of the area *he/she* (and the family) will be moving to.
- A candle with a suitable design made by the congregation.
- A holding cross.
- A card that everyone has signed.

Blessing

Before the service, ask members of the congregation to read a part of the blessing so, as they are surrounded by a circle of people, the ordinand (and family) will also be surrounded by the words of blessing.

Invite all the members of the congregation to come forward and surround the ordinand (and family). Everyone might stretch out their hands towards the ordinand.

Voice 1	May God bless you in your going from here.
Voice 2	May God bless you in your arrival there.
Voice 3	May your path be smooth.
Voice 4	May your studies be enriching.
Voice 5	May your time at college be filled with friendships.
Voice 6	May God's love be in all your encounters.
Voice 7	Go from here knowing you take our love and support with you.

Voice 8 gives the final blessing

> May God bless you (*and your family*).
> May Jesus be your companion as you walk this new road.
> May the Holy Spirit stir you up with excitement.
> Go from here knowing you are loved by us and by God.
> Go very well!
> **Amen**

Songs

Do not be afraid
(*Hymns Old and New: New Anglican Edition*)

I, the Lord of sea and sky
(*Hymns Old and New: New Anglican Edition*)

I want to serve the purpose of God (In my generation)
(*The Source 3*)

My Jesus, my Saviour (Shout to the Lord)
(*Hymns Old and New: One Church, One Faith, One Lord*)

One is the body
(*One Is the Body*)

You are called to tell the story
(*Hymns of Glory, Songs of Praise*)

Action

Decorate a candle with words *(see How to Put a Design onto a Candle on page 209)*. Suggested words could be:
    'May God's light show you the way'
    'May God bless you and keep you'
    'Lighten our darkness'
    'Here I am, Lord'

Print a card and ask everyone to sign it *(see design on page 159)*.

CARD FOR ORDINAND STARTING TRAINING

Farewell to a Person Departing for a Mission Overseas

Ask the person to come to the front. Introduce them and ask them where they are going, what they will be doing and something about the organization they are attached to. If a family are travelling abroad you might talk about plans for living and schooling.

Prayer

Lord, we gather today not only to worship you but to pray for N as *he/she* answers your call to do your work in *place*. We pray that you will uphold N in the planning and preparation for the journey. We pray for the people waiting for N as they open their hearts and homes in welcome. And we ask that your Holy Spirit will move between N and the people *he/she* will encounter during *his/her* work that your kingdom of love and justice and peace will spread to all who seek to know you.
Amen

Bag for Life

N is presented with a Bag for Life. Members of the congregation come forward, each holding something that might be useful while N is away from home. Items may include chocolate, teabags, favourite food it might be difficult to obtain where the person is going, an international phone card, a list of essential home phone numbers, email addresses, a group photo of church friends, a signed card, a map, a small Bible, a prayer book, a small cross, a candle. Each item is presented to N and placed in the Bag for Life with appropriate words:

> Here is chocolate for emergencies.
> Here is a phone card to help you keep in touch.
> Here is a list of phone numbers you might need.
> Here is a list of friends' email addresses.

Here is a photo to remind you of your friends here.
Here is a card signed by us all.
Here is a map of *place*.
Here is a small Bible to carry with you.
Here is a prayer book to help you pray.
Here is a cross to carry in your pocket.
Here is a candle to light your path.

Blessing

The ministry team and friends of N come forward and surround N. They may like to lay their hands on N.

N, as you leave this place and journey to another,
May God go with you and keep you safe.

As you meet new people and new situations,
May Jesus protect and guide you.

In your words and your work,
and your mission in *place* to further God's kingdom,
May the Holy Spirit inspire you.

And, until we meet again,
may the blessing of God almighty,
the Father, the Son, and the Holy Spirit,
be with you today and always.
Amen

Songs   **Be with me, Lord (Psalm 91)**
(*Cantate*)

God of mission, still you send us
(*New Start Hymns and Songs*)

God's Spirit is in my heart
(*Hymns Old and New: New Anglican Edition*)

I will be with you
(*Be Still and Know*)

May the peace of the Lord Christ go with you
(*Celtic Hymn Book*)

Sent by the Lord am I
(*Hymns of Glory, Songs of Praise*)

Action

Make and fill a Bag for Life *(see How to Make on page 207)* and stock up on appropriate contents.

Print a card and ask everyone to sign it *(see design on page 163).*

Organize a rota of church members who will undertake to write a letter or email each week or month to N while *he/she* is away so that *he/she* has regular news from home. This can be a vital lifeline when someone is in a remote place.

CARD FOR PERSON LEAVING FOR MISSION OVERSEAS

Welcome and Commissioning of a New Pastoral Assistant

Song   **Christ has no hands but ours**
Martin Foster – sheet music available from Bear Music, 3 Beech Court, River Reach, Teddington, TW11 9QW

After the song, ask the pastoral assistant to come to the front. Introduce him/her and talk a bit about the training and authorization service that has taken place

Introduction   The office of pastoral assistant in this diocese is a recognized form of ministry supporting the whole ministry of God's people. It is an honourable one, having roots in the life of the early Church, supporting both the baptized and ordained ministry of the Church in the proclamation of the Good News, and in the care of all God's people. We gather here to commission N that *her/his* ministry may be both recognized and blessed, in order that the work of the Church in this place may be both strengthened and advanced.

The Charge   N, will you be faithful in the ministry of pastoral care in this place that the work of the Church may be strengthened and advanced?

I will.

Will you, through worship, prayer, study and witness, seek to reflect the Good News of Jesus Christ, to the praise of the Father and through the inspiration of the Holy Spirit?

I will.

Will you, the people of God gathered in this place, support *N* by your prayers and with your friendship?

We will.

The Commission   This is the day the Lord has made.
Let us rejoice and be glad in it!

Give to your servant *N* the gifts of faith, hope and love, that *he/she* may execute the office of pastoral assistant in this place, to your praise and honour.

May *his/her* hands be ready to do your work.
May *his/her* eyes be open to recognize those in need.
May *his/her* ears hear soft-spoken words of pain or sorrow.
May *his/her* voice speak of healing and peace.
May *his/her* feet walk the extra mile with those who falter.
And may *he/she* always be aware of your presence guiding *him/her* and your loving protection around *him/her*
in all that *he/she* does.
Amen

Other pastoral assistants in the church are invited forward to join N and N is presented with a gift.

Blessing   May the blessing of God the Father, God the Son, and God the Holy Spirit, rest upon you and your ministry, this day and for evermore.
Amen

The sharing of the Peace may follow and then all return to their seats before one of the following songs (or another) is sung.

Song   **Christ's is the world (A touching place)**
(*Hymns Old and New: New Anglican Edition*)

OR

Longing for light (Christ, be our light)
(*Christ, Be Our Light* or *Laudate*)

OR

Lord, make us servants of your peace
(*Hymns of Glory, Songs of Praise*)

Action   A presentation gift – this might be a pastoral book, a book on prayer, a Bible or a candle, or something appropriate to the person's ministry.

The Introduction and Charge are © Paul Jenkins 2003 using words adapted from Common Worship.

Welcome to a New Curate

When a new curate arrives in a parish, there will have been an ordination service in the cathedral, which will have been planned by the diocese. Some of the congregation may have gone to this service, but the first Sunday after the ordination is the time for the parish to officially welcome the new curate and *his/her* family.

Before the curate moves into *his/her* new house the parish might offer help with cleaning and decorating. Once the curate has moved into the house, which may well be a few weeks before the ordination, it is good if some members of the parish can pop around to say hello and introduce themselves, taking a meal, a cake, or offering to help with anything to make them feel at home.

Do remember that the curate will go on retreat for a few days leading up to the ordination. If *he/she* has come with a family, the family will be left alone for these few days. If the couple have journeyed together through training, some spouses may find it hard not being involved in this final preparation. If the diocese offers any retreat time to the spouses of the ordained, do offer help with babysitting so they can go along.

Some Ideas for the First Service

Present the new curate with a Knowledge File. The parish can put together such a file about the local community with photos of the people who do the various jobs in the community. This might entail taking pictures of the places and people 'out there'. As the pictures are taken, the photographer can speak to the people, explaining that the new curate is coming and that the pictures will help the curate to get to know people more quickly. For the new curate to have a collection of pictures of all the people *he/she* might encounter, with their names and what they do, might be really helpful. This file might also include information about the days the bins are emptied, how the papers get delivered, when the milkman delivers, local doctors, dentists, vets and so on – any information that is helpful when moving into a new home in a new area. This information can be used later, to be included in a welcome pack for anyone who moves into the parish and can be taken by the church when they go to welcome newcomers.

If the curate comes with children, a similar leaflet can be put together to welcome the children, including information about any groups the church runs for children, local football clubs and so on. Include information about the local swimming pool, for example, and the times when it is open. Give information about anything that might help the children to settle into the area.

Being a training parish is an important role to be given to a church. It involves both the parish priest and the parish. But, as with all meetings in life, where the trainer and trainee meet is a place of learning for all, so never dismiss the gifts the curate and *his/her* family bring with them. It is important that the church recognizes that the curate and *his/her* family come with past life experience. This is often not recognized. As well as coming for training for the future, the curate also comes with a wealth of experience from their time before ordination. There is an opportunity for this to be recognized in this service. Ask the curate to speak about what *he/she* did before ordination training. If *he/she* is married ask if their spouse would like to speak about their past experience as well.

You might invite the curate and *his/her* family to choose the hymns or songs for the service.

The curate can be given the keys *he/she* will need to have access to the church buildings.

After the service, refreshments can be served so that everyone has a chance to meet the curate and *his/her* family. Do remember that they will be meeting many people and may not remember everyone's name next time they meet, so keep saying who you are for a while!

Welcome to a New Vicar

When a new vicar arrives in a parish, there will be a service which will be planned by the diocese, the area dean, the archdeacon and the bishop's office. The new priest may be involved in choosing the hymns and planning a certain amount of the service. Most dioceses have an approved liturgy that they use, and within that liturgy there is a place where the parish representatives and the local dignitaries welcome the new vicar. Usually these 'welcoming' people come up and shake hands and say a few words, but often there is a feeling that there isn't much time and the service needs to keep moving. Here are a few ideas for this part of the service. This is an opportunity for the church to reach out into the community. The parish priest, along with the bishop, is being given the 'cure of souls' for everyone in the parish, not just those who go to church, so bringing the people 'out there' into the church at this time of welcome is an opportunity not to be missed.

In the Church of England there are basically two forms of service to mark the start of a new ministry within a benefice.

1 When a priest is becoming team rector, rector or vicar, the form of service is an Institution and Induction. The priest must be presented by the patron(s) of the living, is instituted by the bishop and is then inducted and installed by the archdeacon. If the bishop is the patron, the service is a Collation rather than an Institution.
2 When someone is being appointed as team vicar or priest-in-charge, the form of service is a Licensing. The priest may be presented by the patron, is licensed by the bishop and, depending on the circumstances, may be installed by the archdeacon.

The *institution* is the admission by the bishop of a team rector, rector or vicar into the bishop's spiritual oversight and care of a parish or parishes.
The *collation* is the admission by the bishop of a team rector, rector or vicar into the bishop's spiritual oversight and care of a parish or parishes of which the bishop is the patron.

The *induction* is the admission by the archdeacon of a team rector, rector or vicar into the possession of the church building, churchyard and parsonage.

The *licensing* is the admission by the bishop of a priest into the bishop's spiritual oversight and care of a parish or parishes.

The *installation* is the formal placing by the archdeacon of a priest in *his/her* seat in the church.

As well as being welcomed by representatives of groups connected with the church, the vicar might be welcomed by the people in the community who may not be churchgoers, but who consider the vicar and the church to be an important part of their community. This might work particularly well in a rural or suburban parish where the church is used by the local community who live around it. The following people might be asked to be involved:

- local publican/s and restaurant owners
- local shopkeepers
- milkman/woman
- postman/woman
- hairdresser/barber
- heads of local schools
- postmaster/mistress
- builders, plumbers and electricians
- doctors
- undertaker.

These people might bring something to symbolize the work they do in the community.

As each person comes up, they place their symbolic item on the altar or on the floor in front of the altar and go and stand in a semi-circle around the back of the altar. Once everyone has come up they each announce loudly what they do in the community and then they might all welcome the vicar with these words:

We make up the serving community in this place.
We recognize the part the church plays in that community.
We welcome you to join us as we serve the people here together.
We welcome you!
Welcome!

Usually the people who come to welcome the new vicar are adults and people who have status in the community. Perhaps the vicar might also be welcomed by those people who are involved in the day-to-day running of the church and who may not always be fully appreciated. This would illustrate that the body of Christ is made up of everyone, not just the great and the good. Each person who comes up might bring something that symbolizes their role in the church. For example:

- member of choir or music group (a hymn book or musical instrument)
- sacristan (some clean linen)
- cleaners (a duster, pan and brush)
- gardeners (a fork or spade)
- sidespeople (an order of service)
- flower arrangers (a vase)
- coffee makers (a cup and saucer)
- several children (something to represent the different groups of children)
- people who edit the magazine (a copy of the magazine)
- people who clean the silver (a tin of polish)
- people who control the projector or sound system (a microphone)
- people who are involved in house groups or Bible study (a Bible).

As each person comes up, they place their item on the altar or on the floor in front of the altar and then go and stand in a semi-circle around the back of the altar. Once everyone has come up, they each announce loudly what they do in the church and then they might all say this prayer together, or one person might say it, with everyone joining in with the welcome at the end.

> **We each help to make up the body of Christ in this church.**
> **Each doing their small part to make a whole.**
> **With great joy we welcome you to this church as our new vicar.**
> **May your time with us be full of God's love and new adventures together.**
> **You are very welcome!**
> **We welcome you!**

OR

The parish might put together a file about the local community. Include photographs of the places and people who work in the community. Before taking the pictures, explain that the new vicar is coming and that a 'welcome' file will be presented to *him/her*. At the same time give out an invitation to the service and explain that everyone is very welcome to come. It might be very helpful for the new vicar to have a collection of pictures of all the people *he/she* might encounter, with their names and what they do. The file can also include useful information such as the days when the bins are emptied, local doctors, dentist and vets, how to get papers delivered, etc. – information that is needed when someone moves into a new home in a new area. This same information might also be used later to be included in a welcome pack for anyone who moves into the parish, and could be taken by members of the church when they welcome newcomers.

OR

Someone might go around the community with two specially designed cards. One card might have a picture of the new vicar on so people will know what *he/she* looks like, and can give information about the service, and the other card can be for the person to write a message of welcome for the vicar. This card might be an opportunity for the person to write something about what they do in the community *(see designs on pages 173–4)*.

CARD TO WELCOME NEW VICAR

LOCAL BUSINESSES

THE BUTCHER
THE GREENGROCER
THE POST OFFICE
THE CAFE
THE NEWS AGENTS
THE SUPERMARKET
THE BAKER
THE PUB
THE HAIRDRESSER
THE GARAGE

WE WELCOME YOU!

MY NAME IS

MY BUSINESS IS

WE ARE OPEN FROM

WE ARE LOCATED AT

WRITE YOUR MESSAGE TO THE NEW VICAR HERE

CARD FOR NEW VICAR TO HAND OUT TO PEOPLE IN THE COMMUNITY

Stick/cut and paste a picture of the new vicar here

MY NAME IS *insert new vicar's name here*

I AM COMING TO THE PARISH OF *insert the name of the parish here*

TO BE YOUR NEW VICAR

I WILL BE ARRIVING IN THE PARISH ON *insert the date*

THERE WILL BE A SERVICE AT

ST   *insert name of church*   CHURCH

ON *insert date*   TIME *insert time*

PLEASE DO COME TO THE SERVICE

Refreshments will be served afterwards

ALL ARE WELCOME

MY CONTACT DETAILS ARE:

Vicarage address, phone number, email address

Welcome to an Ordinand or Reader in Training on Placement

Welcoming an ordinand or reader in training to a parish as part of their training for ministry is an important moment. The person may feel quite anxious in a place where he or she may know no one. The time spent in a parish with a training incumbent and with the members of the ministry team and congregation can be a defining moment in the person's development and colour much of their early ministry. The welcome to the parish might take place during the Peace or at the end of a main Sunday service, or may be introduced by the following reading.

Reading   *Read by a member of the congregation*

There is one body and one Spirit, just as you were called to the one hope of your calling, one Lord, one faith, one baptism, one God and Father of all, who is above all and through all and in all.

But each of us was given grace according to the measure of Christ's gift.

The gifts he gave were that some would be apostles, some prophets, some evangelists, some pastors and teachers, to equip the saints for the work of ministry, for building up the body of Christ, until all of us come to the unity of the faith and of the knowledge of the Son of God, to maturity, to the measure of the full stature of Christ. We must no longer be children, tossed to and fro and blown about by every wind of doctrine, by people's trickery, by their craftiness in deceitful scheming. But speaking the truth in love, we must grow up in every way into him who is the head, into Christ, from whom the whole body, joined and knitted together by every ligament with which it is equipped, as each part is working properly, promotes the body's growth in building itself up in love.

Ephesians 4.4–7, 11–16

Dialogue

The minister asks the person to come forward and introduces him/her to the congregation, explaining that N is on placement with the parish for x weeks/ months as part of his/her training for ordination (or as a reader). N then tells the congregation where he/she is from and what his/her plans are at the end of his/her training. The minister might tell the congregation what N will be doing in the parish during the time of the placement.

Responses

N, as you leave behind all that is familiar in *place*,
and as you begin your ministry in *place*.
We welcome you to our church family.

For the time that lies ahead,
as we work together to further God's kingdom.
We pray for wisdom and an openness of spirit.

For all who answer the call to Christian ministry,
for N's gifts and all *he/she* will share with us.
We give thanks to God.

In our speaking and our doing,
in our listening and our caring,
We pray for God's Holy Spirit to be among us.
Amen

A member of the congregation comes forward to present N with a parish infor- mation pack. This might include the names and contact details of key people, a current parish magazine, a local street map, a calendar of events for the period of N's placement, and other relevant notes

Songs

Alleluia! Raise the Gospel (alternative text)
(*Go Before Us*)

King of kings, majesty
(*The Source 3*)

Let us build a house (All are welcome)
(*Laudate*)

Lord, you have my heart
(*The Source 3*)

One is the body
(*One Is the Body*)

The Church is wherever God's people are praising
(*Hymns of Glory, Songs of Praise*)

Action

Put together an information pack to present to N.

If there is a Sunday school or youth group, ask them to design a welcome card to give to N *(or see design on page 178)*.

Share a cake after the service.

Ask parish group leaders to invite N to meetings and gatherings so that *he/she* gets a good overview of how the parish functions – but be careful not to overwhelm with too much!

WELCOME CARD TO ORDINAND OR READER IN TRAINING ON PLACEMENT

We welcome you into our Church family

Blessing a House

This is a wonderful opportunity to welcome new neighbours, along with family and friends, to a new home.

Give everyone a service sheet.

The Sitting Room *Gather everyone into the sitting room.*

> God of relaxation and rest,
> God of comfort and conversation,
> God of television and music.
>
> Bless all those who gather in this room day by day to unwind and relax.
>
> As the world is brought into the room by the television, let those who watch it be made aware of your creation in all its beauty and pain and sorrow.
>
> May all who stop in this room for a while,
> **know God's love and peace.**

The Kitchen *Gather everyone into the kitchen.*

> God of plenty,
> God of nourishment and drink,
> God of bread broken and wine shared.
>
> Bless all who gather in this room day by day to prepare and share food.
> As the world is brought into this room by the many places where food is grown, make us always aware of the needs of others as we are nourished and sustained by the earth's bounty.
> May all who stop in this room for a while,
> **know God's love and peace.**

A Bedroom   *Gather everyone into a bedroom.*

God of love,
God of rest and sleep,
God of hopes and dreams.

Bless all who will sleep in this house, that they may wake refreshed and ready to celebrate the new day that God has made.
As so many in the world have no roofs over their heads, may we always be grateful for the shelter and warmth that this house provides.

May all who stop in this room for a while,
know God's love and peace.

At the Front Door *Gather everyone at the front door.*

God of welcome,
God of peace,
God of generosity.

Bless all those who pass in and out through this door.
May a warm welcome always be offered and a fond farewell given.
May it be a place of refuge and shelter and may there be an invitation always to return.

May all who pass through this door,
know God's love and peace.

The blessing of God, Father, Son and Holy Spirit, be upon all who will live here and all who will come and visit.
Go in the peace and love of the Lord.
Amen

Action   Ask everyone present to sign a card to give to the house owner, or the house owner might give a card to each person who attends the blessing (*see designs on pages 181–2*).

CARD FOR HOUSE BLESSING

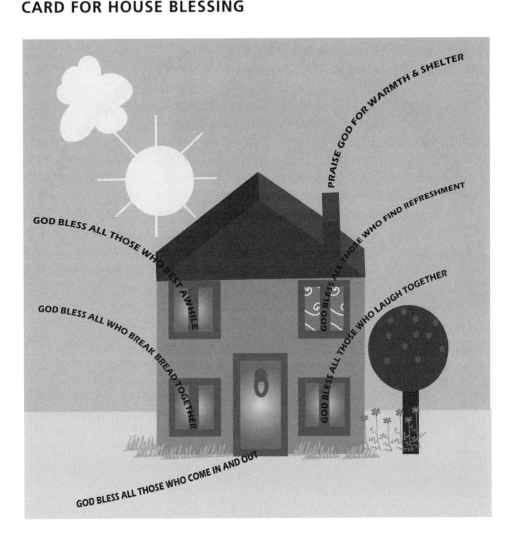

CARD FOR HOUSE BLESSING

BLESS THIS HOUSE AND ALL WHO COME THROUGH ITS DOOR

Thanksgiving and Dedication for a New Building or Re-ordered Church

Here are some resources to use at a service of thanksgiving and dedication for a new building or a re-ordered, or partly re-ordered, church. The words here are adapted from a liturgy used at the opening of a new church hall, and we thank Paul Jenkins for allowing us to adapt and use them.

Opening Responses and Prayer

The stone which the builders rejected has become the headstone of the corner.
This is the Lord's doing: and it is marvellous in our eyes.

This is the day which the Lord has made.
Let us rejoice and be glad in it.

In the name of God, who builds his Church on the foundation of the Apostles and Prophets, Christ himself being the Cornerstone, welcome.
We meet today to give thanks for the completion of our *new building/re-ordered church* and to take part in its dedication.

We honour the vision and foresight of its planners, the skill and dedication of its workers, and the generosity of all who have given both financially and emotionally to make this vision come true. We pray that what is offered here in stone and wood, in glass, metal and fabric, may inspire us and those who come after us in the service of God's people in this community, and in the praise of God's name.

Almighty God, to whose glory we will dedicate this *new building/re-ordered church*, we praise you for the many blessings you have given us; and we pray that all who seek you in this place may find you and, being filled with your Holy Spirit,

may be empowered to do your work, through Jesus Christ our
Lord.
Amen

Anthem

Locus Iste – Bruckner
Locus Iste a Deo factus est inaestimabile sacramentum
irreprehensibilis est.
(This dwelling is God's handiwork; a mystery beyond all price
that cannot be spoken against.)

Readings

'I ask not only on behalf of these, but also on behalf of those
who will believe in me through their word, that they may all be
one. As you, Father, are in me and I am in you, may they also
be in us, so that the world may believe that you have sent me.
The glory that you have given me I have given them, so that
they may be one, as we are one, I in them and you in me, that
they may become completely one, so that the world may know
that you have sent me and have loved them even as you have
loved me. Father, I desire that those also, whom you have given
me, may be with me where I am, to see my glory, which you
have given me because you loved me before the foundation of
the world.'

John 17.20–24

Come to him, a living stone, though rejected by mortals yet
chosen and precious in God's sight, and like living stones, let
yourselves be built into a spiritual house, to be a holy priesthood, to offer spiritual sacrifices acceptable to God through
Jesus Christ. For it stands in scripture:
'See, I am laying in Zion a stone,
a cornerstone chosen and precious;
and whoever believes in him will not be put to shame.'
To you then who believe, he is precious; but for those who do
not believe,
'The stone that the builders rejected
has become the very head of the corner',
and
'A stone that makes them stumble,
and a rock that makes them fall.'

They stumble because they disobey the word, as they were destined to do.

But you are a chosen race, a royal priesthood, a holy nation, God's own people, in order that you may proclaim the mighty acts of him who called you out of darkness into his marvellous light.

Once you were not a people,
but now you are God's people;
once you had not received mercy,
but now you have received mercy.

1 Peter 2.4–10

At the end of the intercessions and Lord's Prayer:

Christ our Cornerstone, set us all close to you as living stones to make a spiritual house for God. We offer our souls and our bodies, our lives and our labours, to be used for your glory, that your kingdom may come.
Amen

If the people are not already in the building to be dedicated, they now move to that place. As they move they might sing, 'One more step along the world I go'.

Dedication   Ever-living Father, watchful and caring, our source and our end, accept us now as we dedicate this *new building/re-ordered church*. May it be a place into which the people of this community find a welcome and may it be a place from which your faithful people here go out to serve their neighbours.

In the faith of Christ and for the benefit of his holy Church we dedicate this *new building/re-ordered church* to the glory of God; in the name of the Father, and of the Son and of the Holy Spirit.

To you, our God and Father, be all honour and glory, now and for ever.
Amen

Songs

Christ is made the sure foundation
(*Hymns Old and New: New Anglican Edition*)

Christ is our corner-stone
(*Common Praise*)

Come, host of heaven's high dwelling place
(*Love from Below*)

Jubilate, everybody
(*Hymns Old and New: New Anglican Edition*)

Let us build a house (All are welcome)
(*Laudate*)

One more step along the world I go
(*Hymns Old and New: New Anglican Edition*)

Closing a Church

The closing of a church is often a very painful time, particularly for those who have worshipped in it and cared for it. It can feel like a huge loss. Sometimes a church is closed and its congregation has to find somewhere new to go, or a church is closed because it is one of a group in the same parish or benefice and maintenance of all the churches is too much to sustain, or sometimes a church is closed because a new church is being built or planned. Whatever the reason for the closing, pain at what is being lost can also be mingled with hope for what is to come, and it is important that the church's final service is planned carefully to reflect a time of ending, as well as anticipating a possible new beginning. The service needs also to reflect that 'the people' are the church, not the building, and therefore the people will continue to be the living church.

CREATIVE IDEAS FOR THE SERVICE

The Celebration

Invite everyone to gather an hour before the service starts to have a final drink and share a cake together. At the end of the service it is important that people feel that the church has closed, and so having refreshments in the church after the service is not helpful. Alternatively, after the service, plan to have refreshments served in another building away from the church. This gives everyone a chance to support each other and discuss what has happened.

Before the final service, ask the congregation to collect together any pictures they have of the church during its lifetime. Make a display out of them.

Invite to the final service people who have been significant in the church's life. This might include past vicars, ministers, and people who have moved away from the area and who have played a part in the church's story. A past vicar might be invited to preach, or instead of the sermon a few people might be invited to speak about an event that they were involved in at the church. This is an opportunity to reach out into the community, so advertise what is happening to people 'out there' and encourage them to come along as well.

The first part of the service needs to be 'upbeat' and a celebration of the church's life up to that point. The prayers and hymns need to have a celebratory feel, giving thanks to God for all that has happened in the church building over the years.

A list of events or names might be read aloud:

- *The names of all those who have married in a given month over the lifetime of the church.*
- *The names of those who have died in a given month over the lifetime of the church.*
- *The names of all those baptized in the church in a given month over the lifetime of the church.*
- *The names of the churchwardens over the lifetime of the church.*
- *The names of the priests or ministers who have served their titles in the church*
- *Significant events.*

These things will all highlight the length of time the church has been there and how many lives the church has touched over the years.

The Ending

Nearing the end of the service the mood changes from one of celebration to one of ending.

During the singing of the last hymn, everyone walks in a procession around the church, stopping at key places. At each place there is a symbolic action to indicate the ending of the use of that thing or place. At each place a different person says the prayer and everyone responds. Either the person who has read the prayer, or a child, then gathers up the relevant item if that is appropriate and takes it on in the procession.

The different places might include the bell tower, the altar, the reserved sacrament (if there is one), the pulpit or lectern, the children's corner, the font, the organ, the choir stalls, the place where refreshment is made and served (if this is in the church), the Mothers' Union banner (or other special banner) and finally out through the main door. The order that this is done in will be determined by the shape and layout of the church.

Choose hymns or songs and readings that reflect endings or being on a journey or which reflect a resurrection theme. Sing the verses as you move from place to place. Here are some ideas:

Lord, you call us to a journey
(*Hymns Old and New: One Church, One Faith, One Lord*)

O Breath of Life
(*Hymns Old and New: New Anglican Edition*)

One more step along the world I go
(*Hymns Old and New: New Anglican Edition*)

Thanks be to God
(*Laudate*)

The Church is wherever God's people are praising
(*Hymns of Glory, Songs of Praise*)

The Spirit lives to set us free (Walk in the light)
(*The Children's Hymn Book*)

THE FINAL JOURNEY AROUND THE CHURCH

The people begin to process around the church, gathering at different points, beginning with the bell tower.

The Bells

Praise the Lord!
Praise God in his sanctuary;
Praise him in his mighty firmament!
(*Psalm 150.1*)

We thank you, Father, for the sound of these bells which ring out your message. As these bells now fall silent, we give thanks for the bell ringers who have faithfully called us to prayer over these many years.

We gather here to celebrate all that has gone before and now we turn towards all that will come.

Ask one of the bell ringers to toll a bell several times. The bell ringers gather photographs or precious items from the bell tower and join the people. A prayer is said.

The Aumbry (or Tabernacle) and the Altar

Jesus took a loaf of bread, and when he had given thanks, he broke it and gave it to them, saying, 'This is my body, which is given for you. Do this in remembrance of me'.
(Luke 22.19)

We thank you, Father, for the many times that bread has been blessed and broken and that wine has been poured and shared at this altar. May we who have been refreshed and nourished Sunday by Sunday go from here with the knowledge that we are your body and your church here on earth.

We gather here to celebrate all that has gone before, and now we turn towards all that will come.

The altar is cleared. Candles blown out, prayer book closed and linen folded. If there is an aumbry or tabernacle, it is emptied and the door left open (see also below). All these things are put in a tidy pile on the cleared altar.

If the church is to be closed and there is no new church to go to, the reserved sacrament is consumed at the last Eucharist conducted in the church, and the door is left open when the altar is stripped. If there is a new church to go to, then the reserved sacrament can be carried to the new church and put on the new altar as a symbol of the continuation from the old to the new.

The candles (reserved sacrament), prayer book and linen are picked up and carried on in the procession either by the person who has read the prayer or by a child.

The Font

Jesus said, 'I am the light of the world.'
(John 8.12)

We thank you, Father, for the myriad of adults and children who have been baptized in this font. We thank you for your ever-growing Christian family. We thank you for the light the members of this family have taken from their baptism out into the wider world.

We gather here to celebrate all that has gone before, and now we turn towards all that is to come.

If there is a lid to the font, it is now put in place. If there is a jug for water, it is picked up and carried on in the procession, either by the person who has read the prayer or by a child.

The Pulpit and Lectern

Jesus said, 'I am the way, and the truth, and the life.'
(John 14.6)

We thank you, Father, for all the words that have been spoken from this pulpit and lectern. For the message of Good News that has been read, the wise words that have been spoken, for learning and explaining, for jokes and laughter, for insight and deeper knowledge. We thank you for the word of God received here in this place.

We gather here to celebrate all that has gone before, and now we turn towards all that is to come.

The Bible on the lectern is closed and carried on in the procession, either by the person who has read the prayer or by a child.

The Children's Corner

This prayer can be read by a child:

Jesus said, 'Let the little children come to me, and do not stop them; for it is to such as these that the kingdom of heaven belongs.' And he laid his hands on them and went on his way.
(Mark 10.14, 16)

We praise God and remember all the children who have played here, all who have laughed and cried here, and all parents who have sat here with their children. We thank you, Father, for all who have taught here and opened the children's minds to God's stories and Jesus' love.

We gather here to celebrate all that has gone before, and now we turn towards all that is to come.

The chairs are stacked onto the tables, some of the children's books and toys are collected together, and artwork is taken off the walls. All these are carried on in the procession either by the person who has read the prayer or by a child.

The Organ and Choir Stalls

Sing to him a new song; play skilfully on the strings, with loud shouts.
(Psalm 33.3)

We thank you, Father, and praise you for the gift of music and singing, and for all those who, over the years, have played the organ. We thank you for all voices raised in praise and thanksgiving, in joy and in sadness. We thank you for the creativity of written music, played and sung, and for all those who have sung in the choir and led the church's singing over many years.

We gather here to celebrate all that has gone before, and now turn towards all that is to come.

The organ hymn book is closed and removed from the organ. The choir hymn books are collected and carried on in the procession either by the person who has read the prayer or by members of the choir.

The Mothers' Union Banner

'My soul magnifies the Lord.'
(Luke 1.46)

We thank you, Father, for the organization of the Mothers' Union worldwide and for this tiny part of it here in N. We praise you and give thanks for all the meetings that have taken place over the years, for the mothers who have come and gone and for the love they have shown their families and friends.

We gather here to celebrate all that has gone before, and now turn towards all that is to come.

The banner is removed from the wall and carried on in the procession by a member of the Mothers' Union.

The place where refreshments are served

Jesus said, 'I am the bread of life.'
(John 6.35)

How blessed we are to have food to make and share, and water to drink. We thank you, Father, for all the fellowship that has been shared, for all the friends made, and for all the cups of tea and coffee that have been drunk.

We gather here to celebrate all that has gone before, and now turn towards all that is to come.

A drying-up cloth is folded, and some cups and saucers are collected together on a tray. These are then carried on in the procession, either by the person who has read the prayer or some of the coffee-makers.

The Main Door

The main door to the church is opened and everyone moves outside. When everyone is outside there is complete silence, and the door is slammed shut very loudly and the key turned in the lock. Allow the silence to continue and then say:

The story of this church is ended. The word has been read, the bread has been broken, the prayers have been offered. It is finished.

The silence continues for a short time.

We have gathered here to celebrate all that has gone before, and now we turn towards all that is to come.

Let us go from here blessed by the gifts this building has given us over these many years, and let us take all the good we have gained from our shared experience forwards to whatever is to come.

The blessing of God, Father, Son and Holy Spirit, be upon all whom you love, all who have worshipped here over the years, and all present here today.
Go in peace to love and serve the Lord.
In the name of Christ.
Amen

Looking Forwards

If there is a new church building, or another church building that will now be used, the procession (if it is near enough) can walk from the old to the new and symbolically place the things taken from the old church into the new. If a new church is to be built, the items removed from the old building can be kept safely and can be part of the opening ceremony of the new church.

HOW TO MAKE

HOW TO MAKE A PAPER ALTAR FRONTAL

1 Take a roll of wallpaper – either lining paper or the reverse side of a patterned paper, the thicker the better. Do not use an embossed paper, as nothing will stick to it.

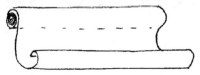

2 Measure the width of the altar and roll out the paper to match. You will need to cut two lengths to make up the height.

3 Stick the middle join together with glue and adjust the height at the middle by overlapping the two sheets of paper. Do not try to cut the paper at the bottom or top, as it is very difficult to cut a straight line. Be careful not to let the glue get on to the front.

4 Turn the paper over so the back is uppermost. Stick brown parcel tape along all the edges and across the middle join – this will stop the edges tearing and strengthen the paper when it is fixed to the altar.

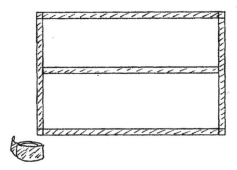

5 Think about how you are going to fix the altar frontal to the altar before you put the design on.

6 Now all you have to do is decorate the front.

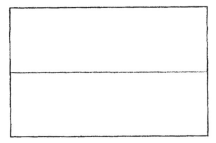

HOW TO DECORATE AN ALTAR FRONTAL WITH THE WORDS 'WE WELCOME YOU'

1 Measure the size needed for the altar frontal (see How to Make a Paper Altar Frontal on page 196).

2 If the frontal is going to be used more than once, then it might be worth making it in window blind fabric as this does not tear.

3 To make the hand stencils:

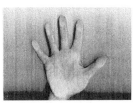

- Photocopy a hand.

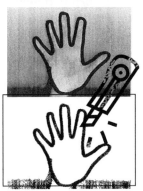

- Draw around the hand with a black pen to give a clear outline. Photocopy onto card.

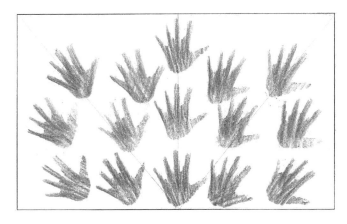

- Using a craft knife, carefully cut around the line to make a stencil of the hand. If more than one person is going to stencil on the hands, then cut out more stencils.

4 Using the hand stencil, put hands all over the background using a water based paint. Start at the bottom with lighter colours, white and yellow, making the colours darker and more orange as the hands get to the top, like a candle flame.

5 Make a stencil of the words 'WE WELCOME YOU' and stencil onto the frontal (see How to Stencil Words onto an Altar Frontal or Banner on page 199).

6 Make a bunting banner of the name of the child to be baptized (see How to Make and Hang Banners on page 202). This goes across the top of the frontal. The frontal now welcomes the child by name for everyone in the church to see. As the name is put on separately, it means the frontal can be personalized and used time and again.

7 Once the frontal is in place, take a photo of it and make it into a card. This can be signed by everyone in church, or if there is a children's group in church the children can sign it and give it to the child. Then the children in the church are welcoming the newly baptized child into their midst.

8 Take a second photo to make into a card to give to the child at the first anniversary of the baptism.

HOW TO STENCIL WORDS ONTO AN ALTAR FRONTAL OR BANNER

1 Measure the size of the altar frontal or banner.
2 Make the background to fit *(see How to Make a Paper Altar Frontal on page 196)*.
3 Measure a piece of thick paper the same size.
4 Using WordArt, or working freehand, draw the letters onto some scrap paper, cut them out and arrange the letters on the thick piece of paper.

5 Draw around the letters and then carefully cut them out with a craft knife.

6 Place the word stencil over the top of the prepared background and stencil the letters on, either with a stencil brush or with spray paint.

7 Put the frontal or banner in place.

HOW TO PUT A DESIGN ONTO AN ALTAR FRONTAL

1 Decide what you want to say on the altar frontal. You might choose some words that are used during the service, SHINE AS A LIGHT IN THE WORLD.
2 Think about the background. Will it be plain, or do you need to put a design on it before putting on the words?
3 Write the words on a computer using a program such as WordArt.
4 Remember that the words need to fit into the space, so choose the font size carefully and think about the shape the words will make and therefore how they will be placed onto the frontal.

HOW TO MAKE AND HANG BANNERS

1 Bunting Banners

You will need a supply of A4 paper.

- Put one letter on each piece of paper. The letters can be printed from a computer using WordArt. Position the letter on the paper so there is room for a 2-inch (5cm) fold at the top of each sheet of paper.
- Make a 2-inch (5cm) fold at the top of each sheet of paper.
- Place a piece of string along the fold and staple the folds down. Make sure not to catch the string in the staples so as to allow the pieces of paper to slide along the string.
- Decorate the letters with hearts, spots and stars. Keep the decorations inside the letters. This is a lovely exercise for children to do. Leave a blank piece of paper between words.

2 Large Banners

Decide how big your banners are going to be. A roll of lining paper can be cut to size. To decorate the banners see instructions for decorating an altar frontal.

The easiest way to hang a large banner is to make a 'tunnel' along the top by folding over the paper or material and fixing in place. To hang the banner up, put a pole through the tunnel. Then either hook up both ends of the pole, or attach string/ ribbon/ cord to either end of the pole and suspend it from a central hook. If there are pillars in the church, the banners can be fixed or hung from these.

EXAMPLES OF BUNTING BANNERS

SHAPES FOR BANNERS

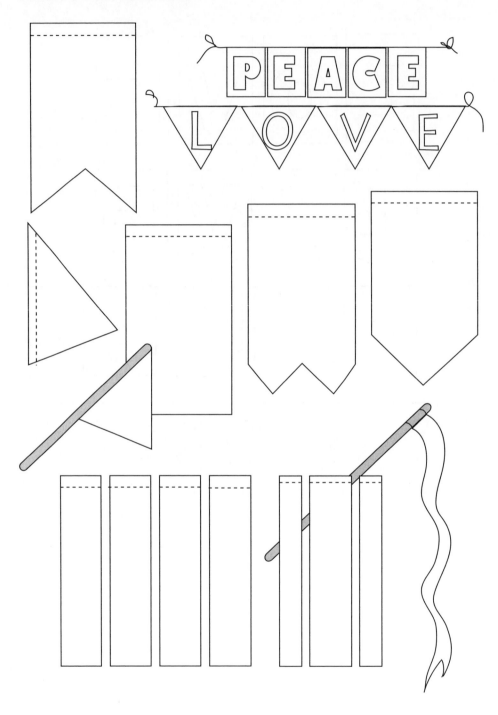

CLOTHING – MAKING A SHAWL FOR WRAPPING THE CHILD/ADULT

1 Cut out a piece of white cotton fabric 45 inches/115cm square for a child or 60 inches/150cm square for an adult.
2 Using a hot iron, turn over and press the edges in about 2½ inches/6cm twice all the way around, so making a deep hem.
3 Take a piece of paper and practise writing with a simple style slightly smaller than the hem, using suitable 'wrapping words'. Repeat on a piece of scrap fabric.
4 Once you feel confident that you can write the words on the cloth, do so all the way around the whole piece of fabric.

HOW TO MAKE A DRAWSTRING BAG FOR CHILDREN

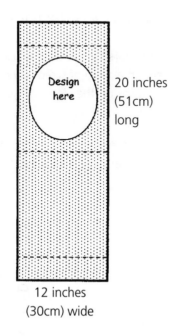

20 inches
(51cm)
long

12 inches
(30cm) wide

1 Cut out a piece of fabric about 20 inches (51cm) long and 12 inches (30cm) wide.
2 If you are going to put a design on the bag, do it now.
3 Make a channel to take the string. Fold the fabric over about 5cm, on both of the short sides, iron it flat and sew along the bottom to make a channel.
4 With the right sides facing, fold the fabric in half in the centre, bringing the two short ends together.
5 Sew up the sides of the bag.
6 Turn the bag round the right way and press the seams flat.
7 Thread the string or cord through the two channels and tie the ends together.

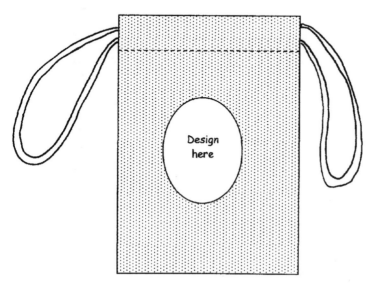

HOW TO MAKE A BAG FOR LIFE

1 Cut out one rectangular piece of plain fabric about 33 inches (84cm) × 16 inches (41cm) for the body of the bag (A).

2 Cut out one piece of fabric about 106 inches (270cm) × 5 inches (12cm) for the handle (B). If necessary this can be made up of pieces of fabric sewn together.

3 Take the large piece of fabric (A) and fold over and sew the two short ends. Iron flat.

4 Take the long piece of fabric (B). Fold over about ½ inch (1 cm) along one long edge and iron flat. Then fold over the other long edge to tuck under the first folded edge. Sew down the centre to catch both the edges. Iron the bag handle flat.

5 Lay the handle along the right side of the bag as shown, starting and finishing at the centre fold of the bag. Pin in place, making a complete circle, and then sew the handle onto the bag.

6 Write **BAG FOR LIFE** on the bag.

7 Turn the bag right sides together and sew down the two side edges.

8 Turn the bag round the right way and press the edges.

9 The bag is now ready to be filled.

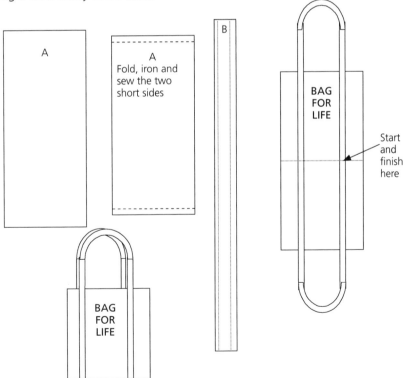

HOW TO PUT A DESIGN ONTO FABRIC USING APPLIQUÉ

1 Measure and cut out the background fabric. If needed, stiffen fabric with iron-on stiffener.

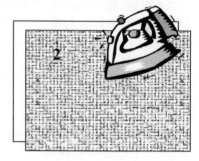

2 Choose the fabric to be sewn onto the background. Iron a piece of stiffener onto the back of the fabric.

3 Place the shape to be used onto the stiffener and cut the shape out.

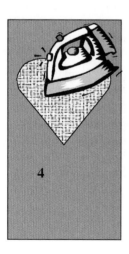

4 Place a piece of 'wonderweb' between the cut-out shape and the background and iron on. This keeps the shape in position when it is being sewn onto the background.

5 Sew the shape onto the background.

HOW TO PUT A DESIGN ONTO A CANDLE

Putting a design onto a candle is simple, but may need a little practice. Working on a rounded surface can be quite difficult the first time it is tried. Square candles are easier to work on. The bigger the candle, the easier it is to put on the design – very thin ones have little surface to work on.

1 First buy the candle, bearing in mind where it is to go and what the design is to be.
2 Decide on the colours to be used.
3 Work out the design to go on the candle, keeping it very simple.
4 Wrap a piece of paper round the candle to see how big the design should be and how it will be positioned on the candle. Most candles will only be seen from one side, so remember to design the candle with that in mind.
5 Now draw the design on the same piece of paper with a strong line. (If drawing is too difficult, use a computer to type and print off words in a big bold font.)
6 Put sellotape onto the top and bottom of the design paper and stick in place on the candle.
7 With a biro or pencil go over the design and gently press the design into the candle surface.
8 Take the paper off the candle and the design should be visible on the surface.
9 With a waterproof felt pen fill in the design.
10 Using relief outliner made to use on glass, go round the outline of the design.
11 Leave to dry.

Decorating a candle using shapes cut from wax sheets

Thin coloured sheets of wax can be bought from an art and craft supplier such as Opitec <www.opitec.co.uk>. Cut shapes or letters out of the wax to decorate a candle. You can draw your own templates or buy shaped cutters from a supplier such as Opitec, or use shaped metal or plastic biscuit or pastry cutters easily found in cook shops that supply cake decoration materials. The shapes can be gently pressed onto the candle in position. This is a wonderful way to add an extra design to a candle.

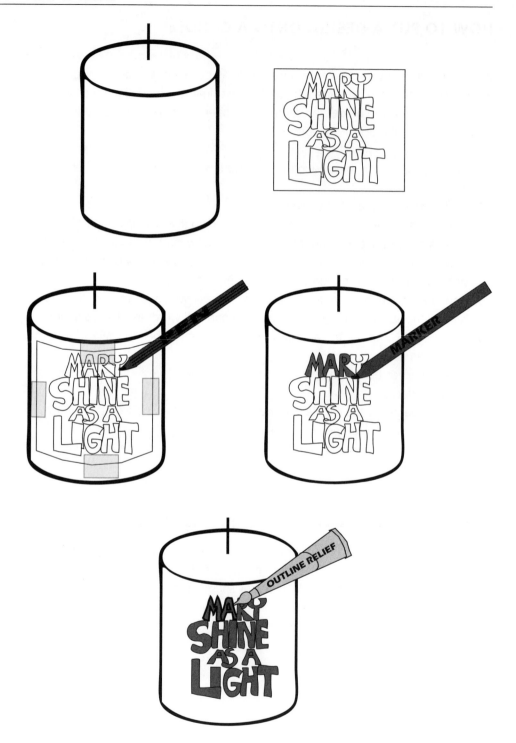

HOW TO MAKE A STOLE

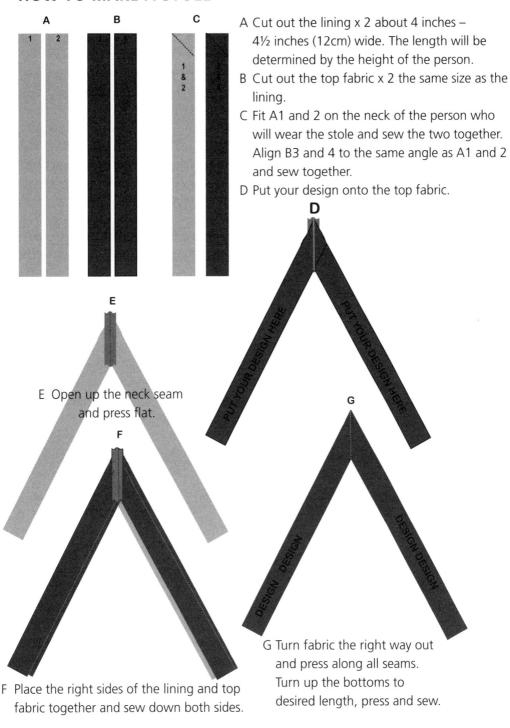

A Cut out the lining x 2 about 4 inches – 4½ inches (12cm) wide. The length will be determined by the height of the person.

B Cut out the top fabric x 2 the same size as the lining.

C Fit A1 and 2 on the neck of the person who will wear the stole and sew the two together. Align B3 and 4 to the same angle as A1 and 2 and sew together.

D Put your design onto the top fabric.

E Open up the neck seam and press flat.

F Place the right sides of the lining and top fabric together and sew down both sides.

G Turn fabric the right way out and press along all seams. Turn up the bottoms to desired length, press and sew.

RESOURCES FOR CREATING SERVICES

HYMNS AND SONGS

Be Still and Know

Give me, Lord, a new heart
I received the living God
I will be with you
Jesu Domine
Jesus, ever-flowing fountain
Listen, let your heart keep seeking
Lord Jesus Christ, your light shines
May the Lord bless you
My peace
Nada te turbe (Nothing can trouble)
O the word of my Lord
O, the love of my Lord (As gentle as silence)
Silent, surrendered
Take my hands
Veni, lumen cordium (Come, light of our hearts)
Veni, Sancte Spiritus (Come, Holy Spirit)
You are the centre

Cantate

A lamp for my feet (Psalm 119)
Be with me, Lord (Psalm 91)
Bread of life from heaven
Go in peace
God is forgiveness
I will walk in the presence of God
I'll follow my Lord
Jesus, Saviour (Psalm 25)

Let us go in peace
Litany and Prayers (Holden Evening Prayer)
May the Word of God strengthen us
My heart is searching (Psalm 63)
O Word of God
Over my head
Send down the fire
Word of God

Celebration Hymnal for Everyone

Baptised in water
Father, in my life I see
Flow, river, flow
Follow me, follow me
God, our fountain of salvation
Here's a child for you, O Lord
If you would follow me
O God, I seek you
O Lord, you are the centre of my life
Out of darkness God has called us
Praise to you, O Christ our Saviour
Send forth your Spirit, O Lord
Though the mountains may fall
We are called
You have put on Christ
You shall cross the barren desert

Celtic Hymn Book

Be thou a smooth way
Christ be with me
Christ be beside me
Come and find the quiet centre
Come my Lord, my light, my way
Empty, broken, here I stand
How good it is to know your name
I give myself to you, Lord
In our journeying this day

In the power of the Creator
Jesus, draw me ever nearer
May the peace of the Lord Christ go with you
The peace of the earth
This day God gives me
Those who live in God's own shelter
Through the love of God our Saviour
You are the peace of all things calm
You, Lord, are in this place

Christ, Be Our Light

I rejoiced
Let nothing trouble you
Longing for light (Christ, be our light)
O God, you search me
On the day I called

Come All You People

Behold, I make all things new
Don't be afraid
I am the vine
Send out your light
Take, O take me as I am

Common Ground

Come and gather round
Mallaig Sprinkling Song
Now through the grace of God
Spirit of God, unseen as the wind
Tree of Life and awesome mystery
Will you come and follow me

Common Praise

Christ is our corner-stone
Eternal God, we consecrate

God the Father, name we treasure
Holy Spirit, come confirm us
O thou who camest from above
There's a spirit in the air
We bring our children, Lord, today

Complete Anglican Hymns Old and New

Breathe on me, breath of God
Father God, I wonder
Gifts of bread and wine
My God, accept my heart this day
O let the Son of God enfold you
Spirit of the living God

Enemy of Apathy

Lo, I am with you
The love of God comes close

Go Before Us

Alleluia! Raise the Gospel
Alleluia! Raise the Gospel (alternative text)
Christ beside us
Come to the well
Community of Christ
If today you hear God's voice
My soul is thirsting
Take my gifts
Word of God

God Beyond All Names

God has chosen me
God of Abraham (Litany)
God, beyond our dreams (God, beyond all names)

Heaven Shall Not Wait

Oh where are you going?
Sing hey for the carpenter
The strangest of saints

Hymns and Psalms

A mighty mystery we set forth
Just as I am, without one plea
Lord Jesus, once a child
Lord, look upon this helpless child
Lord, we have come at your own invitation
Now in the name of him who sent
This child from God above

Hymns of Glory, Songs of Praise

A little child the Saviour came
All I once held dear
All that I am, all that I do
As a fire is meant for burning
Blest are they, the poor in spirit
Child of blessing, child of promise
Courage, brother! Do not stumble
For me to live is Christ
God in such love for us lent us this planet
Halle, halle, hallelujah! (O God, to whom shall we go?)
Here is the place, now is the time
Holy Spirit, gift bestower
I bind my heart this tide
I bind unto myself today
I want Jesus to walk with me
Jesus, I come trusting your kindness
Like the murmur of a dove's song
Lord, make us servants of your peace
Loving Spirit, loving Spirit
Moved by the Gospel, let us move
O holy dove of God descending

Put peace into each other's hands
Sent by the Lord am I
She sits like a bird, brooding on the waters
Take my life, Lord, let it be
The Church is wherever God's people are praising
This is a day of new beginnings
This is the body of Christ
Thuma mina (Send me, Lord)
When I needed a neighbour
You are called to tell the story

Hymns Old and New: New Anglican Edition

All things bright and beautiful
Alleluia, alleluia, hearts to heaven and voices raise
Be thou my vision
Broken for me, broken for you
Christ is made the sure foundation
Christ's is the world (A touching place)
Come Holy Ghost, our souls inspire
Do not be afraid
God forgave my sin (Freely, freely)
God's Spirit is in my heart
I come with joy
I, the Lord of sea and sky (Here I am, Lord)
Jesus put this song into our hearts
Jubilate, everybody
Let there be love
Lift high the Cross
Lord, for the years
O Breath of Life
O Jesus, I have promised
One more step along the world I go
When God Almighty came to earth (God on earth)
You shall go out with joy

Hymns Old and New: One Church, One Faith, One Lord

A new commandment

Amazing grace
Be still and know that I am God
Be still, for the presence of the Lord
Brother, sister, let me serve you
For I'm building a people of power
Forth in the peace of Christ we go
Go peaceful, in gentleness
God is here! As we his people
I heard the voice of Jesus say
If you believe and I believe
Jesu, Jesu, fill us with your love
Jesus, be the centre (Be the centre)
Lord of creation, to you be all praise!
Lord, the light of your love (Shine, Jesus, shine)
Lord, you call us to a journey
Make me a channel of your peace
My Jesus, my Saviour (Shout to the Lord)
Peace, perfect peace, is the gift
Teach me to dance
The King of love my shepherd is

I Will Not Sing Alone

I will sing a song of love
Jesus Christ, here among us
Were I the perfect child

Iona Abbey Music Book

Gifts of the Spirit (When our Lord walked the earth)
God beyond knowledge
God to enfold you
Inspired by love and anger
Jesus calls us here to meet him
Sing for God's glory
Sisters and brothers, with one voice
Take this moment
The God of heaven (Heaven on earth)
The love burning deep (Come out of the darkness)

The love of God comes close
Today I awake
We rejoice to be God's chosen
Yearnings (We bring our yearnings, Lord)

Laudate

Eat this bread
God, at creation's dawn
Here in this place (Gather us in)
I saw streams of water flowing
Into the family of God
Let us build a house (All are welcome)
Lord, as the day begins
Love from below
May you walk with Christ beside you
O come let us follow
Shepherd me, O God
Songs of thankfulness and praise
Thanks be to God
Up from the waters
We are God's work of art
We are many parts
We walk by faith
With joy you shall draw water
You who dwell in the shelter of the Lord (On Eagle's Wings)

Liturgical Hymns Old and New

Lord, for tomorrow and its needs
O, come to the water
Springs of water, bless the Lord
The light of Christ
There is a river
Walk with me, O my Lord
You have been baptised in Christ

Love from Below

Come, host of heaven's high dwelling place

New Start Hymns and Songs

Christian people, sing together
God of mission, still you send us
God of the passing centuries
Gracious God, in adoration
Living God, your word has called us
Lord, we thank you for the promise
Thanks be to God

One Is the Body

Come and let us worship God
Gifts of the Spirit (When our Lord walked the earth)
Journey prayers
Listen now for the Gospel
One is the body
We will walk with God
You are the God of new beginnings

Rejoice and Sing

At the dawning of creation
To Abraham and Sarah
We praise you, Lord, for Jesus Christ
Word of the Father, the life of creation

Restless Is the Heart

Come to set us free
Everyday God
Give us, Lord, a new heart
Jesus, you are the bread we long for
Jubilee Song

Share the Light

Share the light
The peace of God
There is someone
Though we are many/Make us a sign
You have called us

Sing Glory

All that I am
Because the Lord is my shepherd
Born by the Holy Spirit's breath
Christ is made the sure foundation
Church of God, elect and glorious
Come, light of the world
Come, now is the time to worship
Come, O Holy Spirit, come (Wa wa wa Emimimo)
Faithful One
Forth in your name, O Lord, I go
Here on the threshold
Lead me, Lord
Lord, bless and keep this little child
Spirit of Jesus
The Lord's my shepherd (Townend)
This is the truth which we proclaim
To be in your presence
We are marching

Songs and Prayers from Taizé

Bless the Lord
Come and fill (Confitemini Domino)
In the Lord
O Lord, hear my prayer
Spirit of Christ Jesus (Spiritus Jesu Christi)
The Lord is my light
Veni Sancte Spiritus (Come, Holy Spirit)

Songs of Fellowship

Father, we adore you (Fountain of life)
I am a new creation
I want to serve the purpose of God (In my generation)
I'm accepted, I'm forgiven
Reign in me
Spirit, breathe on us
You are the vine

The Children's Hymn Book

Abba, Father, let me be
Be the centre of my life
Bind us together, Lord
Don't build your house on the sandy land
Each of us is a living stone (Living stones)
Father welcomes all his children
Father, I place into your hands
Father, we adore you
Have you heard the raindrops (Water of life)
He's got the whole world in his hand
I will sing, I will sing
Isn't it good
Seek ye first the kingdom of God
The King is among us
The Spirit lives to set us free (Walk in the light)
The wise man built his house upon a rock
There are hundreds of sparrows

The Source 3

All to Jesus I surrender
As we are gathered
Beauty for brokenness (God of the poor)
Change my heart, O God
Father in heaven, how we love you (Blessed be the Lord God Almighty)
Filled with compassion (For all the people who live on the earth)
From heaven you came (The Servant King)

Here is bread
I want to serve the purpose of God (In my generation)
I will offer up my life (This thankful heart)
Jesus, take me as I am
King of kings, majesty
Lord, I come to you (Power of your love)
Lord, you have my heart
O Lord, your tenderness
Only by grace
Overwhelmed by love
Purify my heart (Refiner's fire)
River, wash over me
We'll walk the land (Let the flame burn brighter)

There Is One Among Us

Be still and know (1)
God's eye be within me
In love you summon
Lord of life, we come to you
We will take what you offer

We Walk His Way

Bambelela (Never give up)
Baptised in water
Come to me
God has chosen me
God welcomes all/Amen
Take these words to heart
This we shall do
Wash me in the water
We walk his way
We will be fed with finest wheat

Sheet Music

Available from Decani Music, Oak House, 70 High Street, Brandon, Suffolk.
Child of wonder – Marty Haugen

Come to the river – Bob Hurd
Where your treasure is – Marty Haugen

Sheet Music

Available from Bear Music, 3 Beech Court, River Reach, Teddington, TW11 9QW.

Christ has no hands but ours – Martin Foster

A SELECTION OF HYMN BOOKS AND SONG BOOKS

CDs or cassettes are available for titles marked with an asterisk.

Material by OCP Publications, GIA Publications, the Taizé Community, or Wild Goose Publications, is available from Decani Music. Wild Goose Publications are also available from the Wild Goose Resource Group Online Shop.

Agape: The Stories and the Feast, Marty Haugen, GIA Publications, 1993.
All Are Welcome, Marty Haugen, GIA Publications, 1995.
Anglican Hymns Old and New, compiled by Kevin Mayhew, Kevin Mayhew, 2008.
At the Name of Jesus, Christopher Walker, OCP Publications, 1999.
Be Still and Know, compiled by Margaret Rizza, Kevin Mayhew, 2000.
Cantate: A book of short chants, hymns, responses and litanies, edited by Stephen Dean, Decani Music, 2005.
Carol Praise: A new collection of traditional favourites and contemporary Christmas songs, edited by David Peacock with Noël Tredinnick, Collins, 2006.
Celebration Hymnal for Everyone, edited by Patrick Geary, McCrimmons, 1994.
Celtic Hymn Book, selected by Ray Simpson, Kevin Mayhew, 2005.
Children's Praise, compiled by Greg Leavers and Phil Burt, Marshall Pickering, 1991.
Christ, Be Our Light, Bernadette Farrell, OCP Publications, 1994.
Christe Lux Mundi, music from Taizé Instrumental Edition, Ateliers et Presses de Taizé, GIA Publications, 2007.
Christe Lux Mundi, music from Taizé Vocal Edition, Ateliers et Presses de Taizé, GIA Publications, 2007.
Church Hymnary (fourth edition), editorial panel convened by the Church of Scotland and led by John L. Bell and Charles Robertson, Canterbury Press 2005.

Come All You People, shorter songs for worship, John L. Bell, Wild Goose Publications, 1994.

Common Ground, a song book for all the churches, John L. Bell and Editorial Committee, Saint Andrew Press, 1998.

Common Praise, compiled by Hymns Ancient & Modern Ltd, Canterbury Press, 2000.

Complete Anglican Hymns Old and New, compiled by Geoffrey Moore, Susan Sayers, Michael Forster and Kevin Mayhew, Kevin Mayhew, 2000.

Drawn to the Wonder, hymns and songs from churches worldwide, compiled by Francis Brienen and Maggie Hamilton, Council for World Mission, 1995.

Enemy of Apathy, John L. Bell and Graham Maule, Wild Goose Publications, 1988 (revised 1990).

Fire of Love, Margaret Rizza, Kevin Mayhew, 1998.

Fountain of Life, Margaret Rizza, Kevin Mayhew, 1997.

Gather (second edition), edited by Robert J. Batastini, GIA Publications, 1994.

Gift of God, Marty Haugen, GIA Publications, 2001.

Glory and Praise (second edition), Oregon Catholic Press, 2000.

Go Before Us, Bernadette Farrell, OCP Publications, 2003.

God Beyond All Names, Bernadette Farrell, OCP Publications, 1991.

God's Eye Is On the Sparrow, Bob Hurd and Anawim, OCP Publications, 2002.

Heaven Shall Not Wait, John L. Bell and Graham Maule, Wild Goose Publications, 1987 (reprinted 1994).

Hymns and Psalms, British Methodist Conference, Methodist Publishing House, 1987.

Hymns of Glory, Songs of Praise, editorial panel convened by the Church of Scotland and led by John L. Bell and Charles Robertson, Canterbury Press (on behalf of the Church Hymnary Trust), 2008.

Hymns Old and New (New Anglican Edition), compiled by Geoffrey Moore, Susan Sayers, Michael Forster and Kevin Mayhew, Kevin Mayhew, 1996.

Hymns Old and New: One Church, One Faith, One Lord, compiled by Colin Mawby, Kevin Mayhew, Susan Sayers, Ray Simpson and Stuart Thomas, Kevin Mayhew, 2004.

I Will Not Sing Alone, John L. Bell, Wild Goose Publications, 2004.

In the Sight of the Angels: Psalms, hymns and spiritual songs, Michael Joncas, GIA Publications, 2007.

Instant Hymns: New texts to well-loved tunes, a *Common Worship* resource, Michael Forster, Kevin Mayhew, 2002.

Iona Abbey Music Book: Songs from the Iona Abbey Worship Book, compiled by The Iona Community, Wild Goose Publications, 2003.

*Light In Our Darkness, Margaret Rizza, Kevin Mayhew, 2002.

Laudate, edited by Stephen Dean, Decani Music, 2000.

Liturgical Hymns Old and New, compiled by Robert Kelly, Sister Sheila McGovern SSL, Kevin Mayhew, Father Andrew Moore and Sister Louisa Poole SSL, Kevin Mayhew, 1999.

*Love and Anger: Songs of lively faith and social justice, John L. Bell and Graham Maule, Wild Goose Publications, 1997.

*Love from Below, John L. Bell and Graham Maule, Wild Goose Publications, 1989.

*Many and Great: World Church songs Vol. 1, John L. Bell and Graham Maule, Wild Goose Publications, 1990.

Methodist Hymns Old and New, compiled by Revd Peter Bolt, Revd Amos Cresswell, Mrs Tracy Harding and Revd Ray Short, Kevin Mayhew, 2001.

Mission Praise, compiled by Roland Fudge, Peter Horrobin and Greg Leavers, Marshall Pickering, 1983.

*Morning and Evening: Prayer for the Commute, Prayer for the Journey, Paule Freeburg, DC and Christopher Walker, OCP Publications, 2006.

New Hymns and Worship Songs, Kevin Mayhew, 2001.

New Start Hymns and Songs, compiled by Kevin Mayhew, Kevin Mayhew, 1999.

*One Is the Body: Songs of unity and diversity, John L. Bell, Wild Goose Publications, 2002.

*Psalms of Patience, Protest and Praise: 23 psalm settings, John L. Bell, Wild Goose Publications, 1993.

Rejoice and Sing, Oxford University Press, 1991.

*Restless is the Heart, Bernadette Farrell, OCP Publications, 2000.

*River of Peace, Margaret Rizza, Kevin Mayhew, 1998.

*Sacred Dance: Celtic music from Lindisfarne, Keith Duke, Kevin Mayhew, 2005.

*Sacred Pathway: Celtic songs from Lindisfarne, Keith Duke, Kevin Mayhew, 2004.

*Sacred Weave: Celtic songs from Lindisfarne, Keith Duke, Kevin Mayhew, 2003.

*Sent By the Lord: World Church songs Vol. 2, John L. Bell and Graham Maule, Wild Goose Publications, 1991.

*Share the Light, Bernadette Farrell, OCP Publications, 2000.

Sing! New Words For Worship, Rosalind Brown, Jeremy Davies and Ron Green, Sarum College Press, 2004.

Sing Glory: Hymns, psalms and songs for a new century, edited by Michael Baughen, Kevin Mayhew, 1999.

**Songs and Prayers from Taizé*, Ateliers et Presses de Taizé, Continuum, 1991.

Songs and Prayers from Taizé: Cantor and Instruments, Ateliers et Presses de Taizé, GIA Publications, 1991 .

Songs for Prayer, Ateliers et Presses de Taizé, Ateliers et Presses de Taizé, 1998.

Songs for Prayer: Instrumental, Ateliers et Presses de Taizé, Ateliers et Presses de Taizé, 1998.

Songs of God's People, The Panel on Worship, Church of Scotland, Oxford University Press, 1988 (reprinted 1995).

Songs from Taizé, Ateliers et Presses de Taizé, Ateliers et Presses de Taizé, Annually.

Songs of Fellowship, compiled by members of Kingsway Music Editorial Team, Kingsway Music, 1991.

*Tales of Wonder, Marty Haugen, GIA Publications, 1989.

The Children's Hymnbook, compiled by Kevin Mayhew, Kevin Mayhew, 1997.

The New English Hymnal, compiled by Anthony Caesar, Christopher Dearnley, Martin Draper, Michael Fleming, Arthur Hutchings, Colin Roberts and George Timms, Canterbury Press, 1986 (reprinted 1999).

The Source 3: Definitive worship collection, compiled by Graham Kendrick, Kevin Mayhew, 2005.

**There Is One Among Us: Shorter songs for worship*, John L. Bell, Wild Goose Publications, 1998.

*Walk with Christ, Stephen Dean, OCP Publications, 1996.

**We Walk His Way: Shorter songs for worship*, John L. Bell, Wild Goose Publications, 2008.

World Praise, David Peacock and Geoff Weaver, Marshall Pickering, 1993.

Worship (third edition), edited by Robert J. Batastini, GIA Publications Inc., 1986.

21st Century Folk Hymnal, compiled by Kevin Mayhew, Kevin Mayhew, 1999.

A SELECTION OF
RESOURCE BOOKS

A Book of Blessings, compiled and written by Nick Aiken and Alan Elkins, SPCK, 2009.

A Child's Baptism in the Church of England: A guide for parents and godparents, Church House Publishing, 2007.

A Place at the Table: Liturgies and resources for Christ-centred hospitality, Dilly Baker, Canterbury Press, 2008.

A Wee Worship Book, Wild Goose Worship Group, Wild Goose Publications, 1999.

At the Cutting Edge: A prayer manual for young people, Nick Aiken and Tim Sudworth, Canterbury Press, 2003.

Baptism: Its purpose, practice and power, Michael Green, Authentic Media, 2006.

Baptism Matters, Nick and Hazel Whitehead, Church House Publishing, 2004.

Becoming a Godparent: A guide for godparents and parents, Church House Publishing, 2007.

Becoming a Godparent in the Church of England, The Archbishops' Council, Church House Publishing, 2003.

Being Confirmed, Nick Aiken, SPCK, 2004.

Bread for the Journey: Reflections for every day of the year, Henri J. M. Nouwen, Darton, Longman & Todd, 1996.

Celtic Worship Through the Year, Ray Simpson, Hodder & Stoughton, 1997.

Common Worship: Christian initiation, Church House Publishing, 2006.

Common Worship: Daily prayer, Church House Publishing, 2005.

Common Worship: Pastoral services (second edition), Liturgical Commission, Church House Publishing, 2004.

Confirmation: Bible readings for special times, Mike Starkey, Bible Reading Fellowship, 2006.

Confirmation Notebook, compiled by Hugh Montefiore, SPCK, 2002.

Confirmation Prayer Book, Stephen Lake, SPCK, 2002.

Connecting with Baptism: A practical guide to Christian initiation today, edited by Mark Earey, Trevor Lloyd and Ian Tarrant, Church House Publishing, 2007.

Crafts for Creative Worship: A resource and activity book for parishes, Jan Brind and Tessa Wilkinson, Canterbury Press, 2004.

Creating Uncommon Worship, Richard Giles, Canterbury Press, 2004.

Creative Ideas for Evening Prayer: For seasons, feasts and special occasions, Jan Brind and Tessa Wilkinson, Canterbury Press, 2005.

Creative Ideas for Pastoral Liturgy: Funeral, thanksgiving and memorial services, Jan Brind and Tessa Wilkinson, Canterbury Press, 2008.

Creative Ideas for Quiet Days: Resources and liturgies for retreats and days of reflection, Sue Pickering, Canterbury Press, 2006.

Faith Confirmed, Peter Jackson and Chris Wright, SPCK, 1999.

Family Prayers, Nick Aiken and Rowan Williams, Paulist Press, 2002.

Hay and Stardust: Resources for Christmas to Candlemas, Ruth Burgess, Wild Goose Publications, 2005.

Holy Ground: Liturgies and worship resources for an engaged spirituality, Neil Paynter and Helen Boothroyd, Wild Goose Publications, 2005.

In this Hour: Liturgies for pausing, Dorothy McRae-McMahon, SPCK, 2001.

Iona Abbey Worship Book, compiled by The Iona Community, Wild Goose Publications, 2001.

Liturgies for the Journey Of Life, Dorothy McRae-McMahon, SPCK, 2000.

Making Liturgy: Creating rituals for worship and life, edited by Dorothea McEwan, Pat Pinsent, Ianthe Pratt and Veronica Seddon, Canterbury Press, 2001.

Mission-Shaped Children: Moving towards a child-centred church, Margaret Withers, Church House Publishing, 2006.

Mission-Shaped Youth: Rethinking young people and church, Tim Sudworth, Graham Cray and Chris Russell, Church House Publishing, 2007.

Multi-Sensory Church, Sue Wallace, Scripture Union, 2005.

Multi-Sensory Prayer, Sue Wallace, Scripture Union, 2000.

My Baptism Book: A child's guide to baptism, Diana Murrie, Church House Publishing, 2006.

New Patterns for Worship, The Archbishops' Council, Church House Publishing, 2002.

Out of the Ordinary: Prayers, poems and reflections for every season, Joyce Rupp, Ave Maria Press, 2000.

Prayer Rhythms: Fourfold patterns for each day, Ray Simpson, Kevin Mayhew, 2003.

Prayers Encircling the World: An international anthology of 300 contemporary prayers, compiled by SPCK, SPCK, 1998.

Prayers for Life's Particular Moments, Dorothy McRae-McMahon, SPCK, 2001.

Prayers for Teenagers, compiled by Nick Aiken, SPCK, 2003.

Prayers for Your Confirmation, Lois Rock, Lion Hudson, 2007.

Present On Earth: Worship resources on the life of Jesus, Wild Goose Worship Group, Wild Goose Resource Group, Wild Goose Publications, 2002.

Seeing Christ in Others, edited by Geoffrey Duncan, Canterbury Press, 2002.

Stages On the Way: Worship resources for Lent, Holy Week and Easter, Wild Goose Worship Group, Wild Goose Resource Group, Wild Goose Publications, 1998.

The Baptism Cube, Craig Cameron, Church House Publishing, 2006.

The Pilgrims' Manual, Christopher Irvine, Wild Goose Publications, 1997.

The Rhythm of Life: Celtic daily prayer, David Adam, SPCK, 1996.

This Is My Faith: A personal guide to Confirmation and Holy Communion, Douglas Dales, Canterbury Press, 2001.

This Is Our Faith, edited by Jeffrey John, Redemptorist Publications, 1995.

Tides and Seasons: Modern prayers in the Celtic tradition, David Adam, SPCK, 1989.

Times and Seasons: Creating transformative worship throughout the year, Richard Giles, Canterbury Press, 2008.

Times and Seasons: Services and prayers for the Church of England, The Archbishops' Council, Church House Publishing, 2006.

To Serve as Jesus Did, Marty Haugen, GIA Publications, 2005.

Tokens of Trust: An introduction to Christian belief, Rowan Williams, Canterbury Press, 2007.

Using Common Worship: Initiation, Gilly Myers, Church House Publishing and Praxis, 2000.

Watching for the Kingfisher, Ann Lewin, Inspire, 2004.

Words by the Way, Ann Lewin, Inspire, 2005.

Worship Changes Lives: How it works, why it matters, edited by Paul Bradshaw and Peter Moger, Church House Publishing, 2008.

Your Child's Baptism in the Church of England, The Archbishops' Council, Church House Publishing, 2003.

Your Confirmation in the Church Of England: An adult approach to a life of Christian commitment, Stuart Thomas, Kevin Mayhew, 1996.

Youth Emmaus (Emmaus: The Way of Faith), Stephen Cottrell, Sue Mayfield, Tim Sledge, Tony Washington, Church House Publishing, 2003.

Youth Emmaus 2: Big issues and holy spaces, Dot Gosling, Sue Mayfield, Tim Sledge, Tony Washington, Church House Publishing, 2006.

ACKNOWLEDGEMENTS

We would like to thank the following people for giving us permission to include their work in this book.

Andrew Body
For allowing us to include his song 'For the tasks which you are giving'.

Ann Lewin
For allowing us to include 'At a Baptism' from her book *Words By the Way: Ideas and resources for use throughout the Christian Year*, published by Inspire, 2005, and for her continuing supportive interest in our work.

Paul Jenkins
For the Opening Responses to the metrical version of the 'Prayer over the Water', for parts of the liturgy to 'Welcome and Commission a new Pastoral Assistant' using words adapted from *Common Worship*, for allowing us to adapt a liturgy he created for the 'Thanksgiving and Dedication of a New Building or ReOrdered Church', and for being so generous with his support and advice.

St Peter's Church, Wolvercote, North Oxford
For allowing us to adapt and include their Baptism leaflet.

We also acknowledge use of the following:

Common Worship: Christian Initiation
We have included some phrases and words from the Baptism and Confirmation liturgy in *Common Worship: Christian Initiation*, published by Church House Publishing, 2006.

Common Worship: Daily Prayer
We have included part of the Prayer of Thanksgiving for Morning Prayer from the day after Ascension Day until the Day of Pentecost from *Common Worship: Daily Prayer*, published by Church House Publishing, 2005.

New Revised Standard Version
Unless otherwise stated, we have taken Bible texts from the New Revised Standard Version of the Bible

What is a Churchwarden?
We have quoted a piece from *What is a Churchwarden?*, published by the Anglican Diocese of Edmonton, Canada, 2006.